The Decline of Local News and Its Impact on Democracy

A study conducted by the League of Women Voters
of Washington Education Fund
November 2022

The nonprofit League of Women Voters of Washington is committed to the mission of defending democracy and empowering voters. We envision a democracy where every person has the desire, the right, the knowledge, and the confidence to participate.

Founded in 1920 out of the suffrage movement, the League is one of the oldest and most respected and recognized nonpartisan organizations in the nation. Year in and year out, the women and men who are members of the League volunteer to provide fact-based information, presentations, and forums to help voters make their own decisions. The positions we hold result from extensive study and reflect the views of our membership.

For media and speaking requests for this study, contact the League at (206) 622-861 or info@lwvwa.org.

The League of Women Voters of Washington
1511 Third Avenue, Suite 900
Seattle, WA 98101
206-622-8961 | www.lwvwa.org

Inside

Preface 4

Executive Summary...6

The Crisis 10

    Numbers don't lie 10

    Ethnic newspapers 19

    Causes 27

    Mis- and disinformation 34

The Impacts 40

    Impact on politics 40

    Impact on civic engagement 45

    Impact on public health 49

    Impact on public finance 53

The Responses 56

    Community partnerships 56

    Nonprofits...59

    Big Tech contributions 61

    Legislation...64

The Future...68

Conclusion...73

Quick Takes...76

A Deeper Dive...80

    The plight of The News Tribune 80

    Rate your local news...82

    Washington Newspapers 2004 vs. 2022 83

    Cascadia Daily News comes to town.....................................87

Newspapers by county...89

Sound Publishing newspapers...92

Observer offers meaty coverage 93

Craigslist, "newspaper killer"...95

Media literacy: Learning what's credible 96

Media Literacy tools 97

Pink slime sites in Washington 98

Publications for WA ethnic communities 99

Washington voting data 2008 to 2021 100

Understanding algorithms 101

Malheur Enterprise digs into finance 102

Will philanthropy save the day?..104

What is nonprofit news? 107

More state nonprofit news outlets......................................107

East Washingtonian: No government aid............................112

Proposed legislation 113

McChesney offers new plan for news 117

Glossary of terms...119

Interviews...121

Charts and graphs 122

Study participants..123

Endnotes..125

Preface

Between 2005 and 2020, one quarter of the nation's newspapers closed, leaving 1,800 communities with no local news outlet. Several national studies have shown the impact of these closures on various aspects of our society, *particularly those that are fundamental to our democratic system of government.*

Until this report, there has been no comprehensive study of the situation as it pertains to Washington state. At the 2021 convention of the League of Women Voters of Washington, delegates authorized a study of the decline of local news in Washington to support League development of a policy position.

The charge of the study committee was to evaluate the condition of news outlets in Washington. Were they disappearing at the same rate as other states? If so, were Washington residents experiencing the same known impacts of lower political participation, less government oversight, higher government costs, reduced community engagement, and a lack of communication about public health? We consider these elements fundamental to our democracy and system of government.

Using standard reporting techniques, committee members gathered information from more than 50 scholars, journalists, elected officials, and government and civic leaders, including public health professionals. The committee also reviewed more than 500 documents, from scholarly studies to articles in the popular press.

Other efforts included tracking circulation and staffing trends within the state, closures of newspapers and the occasional rise of a new outlet. Newspapers with a general population readership as well as those that serve specific ethnic communities were reviewed.

The committee also examined potential measures to protect local news – such as legislation, nonprofit ownership, community partnership, and philanthropy.

The task was not to present solutions. Rather it was to provide information to make readers aware of the significance of the issue with a goal of reaching consensus on a League policy.

Study committee

Dee Anne Finken, co-chair, LWV Clark County
Delores Irwin, co-chair, LWV Kittitas County
Sally Carpenter Hale, LWV Clark County
Linda Hughes, LWV Bellingham-Whatcom County
Joanne Lisosky, Ph.D., LWV Tacoma-Pierce County
Carol Rikerd, LWV Tacoma-Pierce County
Lauren Snider, Ph.D., LWV Seattle-King County
Lyn Whitley, LWV Whidbey Island
Sharon Wilhelm, LWV Tacoma-Pierce County

Dee Ann Kline, LWVWA board liaison
Kelly McNabb, graphic artist
Amanda Clark, copy editor

Reading committee

Judie Stanton, chair, LWV Clark County
Lucy Copass, LWV Clallam County
Carolyn Maddux, LWV Mason County

Technical review

William Dietrich, journalist, novelist, assistant professor
Brier Dudley, Seattle Times, Save The Free Press Initiative editor
Benjamin Shors, Washington State University, associate professor
Peggy Watt, Western Washington University, associate professor

How to navigate this report

This report is long. The chief reading device for this report is likely to be electronic rather than print, so here are some ways to make navigation easier.

Clicking on the numbered **endnotes** will toggle back and forth between the text and the numbered source. **A Deeper Dive** contains stories, charts and graphs to help illustrate and reinforce points in the body of the report. There are interior links to take you to the A Deeper Dive entries that apply to relevant sections, and then back to the study.

The four-page **Quick Takes** section summarizes the main points in each chapter.

Brief biographies of the members of the study, reading and technical review committees are <u>here</u>.

Published by League of Women Voters of Washington Education Fund
2023

Executive Summary

The newspaper in your hands is a shadow of its former self. Or perhaps you don't bother with print and check the news on a tablet or smart phone. Or, like millions who choose not to pay for local news, you get a quick take on what's happening in the wider world via an app such as Facebook, Twitter, or TikTok.

Local newspapers – the vehicle millions have relied on for information for important, even critical, life decisions for decades – are in crisis.

Between 2005 and 2020, more than one fourth of the country's newspapers – 2,100 in all – disappeared. Half the journalism jobs went away. So did half of the newspaper subscribers. The losses left residents of 1,800 communities in news deserts, meaning they had no local newspaper.

This data is from Penelope Muse Abernathy, a former journalist and now a faculty member at the University of North Carolina and a visiting professor at Northwestern University Medill School of Journalism.[1]

Abernathy's research represents some of the most comprehensive reporting on the crisis. She is the author of five major research projects on the topic, the most recent published June 29, 2022. In that publication, Abernathy updated the decline: "Newspapers are continuing to vanish at a rapid rate. An average of more than two a week are disappearing." That means the country is on track to lose a third of its newspapers by 2025.

Do You Live in a News Desert?

■ No Newspapers
■ One Newspaper

In the U.S. 200 counties do not have a local newspaper. Half of all counties - 1,540 - have only one newspaper, usually a weekly.

Source: UNC Hussman School of Journalism and Media

Figure 1

Why is that important?

Even before our country's founding, newspapers were a cornerstone of civic lives. Newspapers provided information that enabled readers to be involved in efforts to grow our fledgling democracy. Over the centuries, newspapers have continued to educate readers about significant issues, including providing information so that we could select leaders to help us build healthy and productive communities.

In subsequent years the media landscape has changed dramatically. The influence of radio and televised news broadcasts and more recent forms of communication like online news sites, blogs, and social media has further shaped how Americans access news and information. Expanding the formats and sources of news has masked the real disappearance of newspapers.

National research shows the loss of newspapers over the past 20 years has caused serious impacts: Fewer people running for office and fewer people voting, less community engagement, increased political partisanship, and negative outcomes in public health and public finance, among other concerns.

The world, according to the American Press Institute, "is awash in communication."[2] Often these vehicles provide factual, even critical, information.

But some of the information these sources provide isn't journalism. Journalism, according to the institute, is information that features a systematic discipline of verification. That verification not only presents facts, but it presents the truth about the facts.

> "Local newspapers . . . remain, by far, the most significant providers of journalism in their communities."
> —Nieman Lab

Newspapers – with staffing that includes fact-checking editors and reporters who consistently track developments in local government – have been the leading producers of this type of information. Over the years, newspapers have provided more in-depth and continuous reporting on city councils, county councils or county boards of commissioners, health departments, schools and the like. This is known as beat reporting, or "accountability reporting," which, as the American Press Institute explains, is "the work of holding the powerful accountable." Few local television and radio outlets are able to consistently provide this level of reporting.

The focus of this study is on newspapers because of the preeminent role they play. Countless reports support that premise:

"Despite the economic hardships that local newspapers have endured, they remain, by far, the most significant providers of journalism in their communities," according to Duke University researchers Philip M. Napoli and Jessica Mahone. "Essentially, local newspapers produced more of the local reporting in the communities we studied than television, radio, and online-only outlets combined."[3]

A 2011 Federal Communications Commission report also noted that newspapers traditionally have fielded the most reporters in a community and set the agenda for the rest of the local media.[4]

This is a good time to explain this report's use of the term "newspaper." Recognizing the contributions of an increasing number of online-only publications, this study makes use of an inclusive definition. Gig

Harbor Now, a local online-only publication, is considered a newspaper because it provides comprehensive reporting of the area's people, government agencies, schools, and activities.

This report also reflects the thinking of Rob Curley, executive editor of The Spokesman-Review in Spokane. In an interview with Frontline on Dec. 13, 2006, when he was a vice president at The Washington Post, Curley explained, "As long as we understand that the most important part of the word 'newspaper' is 'news' and not 'paper,' we are going to be fine."

Why focus on local newspapers?

The nation's big papers – The New York Times, The Washington Post and The Wall Street Journal – don't provide daily coverage of the communities where most of us live. Unless you live in greater New York City or in or around the nation's capital, you won't learn much from those publications about events and developments that occur near you. And despite the changing media environment, the online circulation of those publications is growing.[5]

This study details efforts to deal with the crisis, including more frequent and thorough online coverage, reductions in print frequency, more robust local coverage, legislation and community fund-raising.

What this study uncovered for Washington

Washington has lost more than two dozen weeklies and three dailies out of the 140 that existed in 2004 – roughly 20% of its newspapers. Again, that compares with a national loss of 25%, which is on track to increase to 33% by 2025.

Staffing declines in Washington are greater than the nationwide average. According to Abernathy, newsrooms nationwide have lost more than 50% of their staff. In Washington, Sen. Maria Cantwell reports newsroom losses of 67%.

Both nationally and in Washington, coverage has shrunk dramatically. In perhaps the most egregious case, the newsroom staff at The News Tribune in Tacoma, purchased a few years ago by a hedge fund, declined from more than 120 employees to just over more than two dozen.

More than half of the nation's dailies are owned by large chains, many indebted to finance firms. In Washington, six papers are owned by a hedge fund and all but one have experienced drastic circulation declines. Particularly distressing is the story at two Chatham Asset Management-owned papers: The Olympian, serving the state capital, and The News Tribune, which serves the state's second most populated county.

Like those across the country, Washington newspapers are suffering because their funding models collapsed in the wake of the expansion and popularity of the internet and Big Tech, including Facebook, Google and Microsoft.

What is the impact?

As is the case throughout the nation, the decline has meant Washington, too, is experiencing an explosion of mis- and disinformation, creating significant challenges for public health officials and others. Coverage of government agencies and elected officials in Washington has dropped significantly, as well.

Those changes apparently have been a relief to some officials, but are concerning to the more conscientious. How do people know, for instance, about inappropriate behavior by those in power? Or about a lack of adherence to regulations? Or about construction projects where corners have been cut?

How do people know where to locate the latest vaccine to combat a public health crisis or for support for children whose lives have become chaotic because of a pandemic?

National studies link a drop in voter participation to the newspaper decline. Original research by the news study committee found a similar outcome for Washington. The decline also has meant less community engagement and greater political partisanship. Observers lament the loss of the souls of communities and the glue that holds communities together.

> "It's not a journalism problem. It's a democracy problem."
> — Benjamin Shors

This study confirmed a troubling reality best described by Benjamin Shors, an associate professor at Washington State University's Edward R. Murrow College of Communication: "This is not a journalism problem. It's a democracy problem."

As the Federal Communications Commission detailed in 2011, people need information about the subjects on which reputable newspapers report: health and welfare, emergencies, jobs and businesses, education, transportation, civics and politics. This information is critical for safe and productive lives in healthy communities.[6]

Our country's founders recognized this reality and enshrined protection for a free press in the U.S. Constitution, and took additional steps beyond that to provide support for it.

"To Benjamin Franklin, Thomas Jefferson, James Madison, and Thomas Paine, 'freedom of the press' did not simply mean that the government would reject censorship," wrote journalists Robert McChesney and John Nichols. "It meant that the government had the fundamental obligation to see that journalism actually existed, that there was something that the government could not censor."[7]

McChesney, whom the committee interviewed, explained: "A free press required a literate population that had ready access to newspapers. For the first several generations of U.S. history, there was no sense at all that journalism could exist on its own courtesy of market forces without enormous government support."

The League values institutions that serve the public good, including libraries, public education systems, public health programs and the justice system.

Newspapers, too, serve the public good.

The Crisis

Numbers don't lie

With apologies to Charles Dickens, this is a tale of two cities and two newspapers, neither of which is experiencing the best of times.

Consider the Yakima Herald-Republic, where upwards of 40 people previously worked in the newsroom. Today, the paper, which serves a city of 96,968 people, has a news staff of 24. (Figure 2)

"In terms of sheer word count, we're not doing as much as before. But we're quicker, providing more context than we have before, and trying to identify the stories the community needs," said executive editor Greg Halling.

To the northwest by about 150 miles, the newsroom at The News Tribune has a staff of 25 to serve Tacoma, population 219,346, more than double that of Yakima, said executive editor Stephanie Pedersen.

In better days, The News Tribune's newsroom staff exceeded 130 people.

In the early 2000s, The News Tribune was "the fastest growing newspaper certainly in Washington state and perhaps on the West Coast," said former publisher David Zeeck. "It's tiny compared to what it was." The effect of the staff reductions is significant and obvious to readers who take close note.

"What's not getting done is the basic bread and butter of local reporting," Zeeck said. "Where we used to cover virtually all of the school boards and any sizable city council, that doesn't happen anymore."

See A Deeper Dive for The plight of The News Tribune
See A Deeper Dive for Rate your local news

Comparing two newspapers

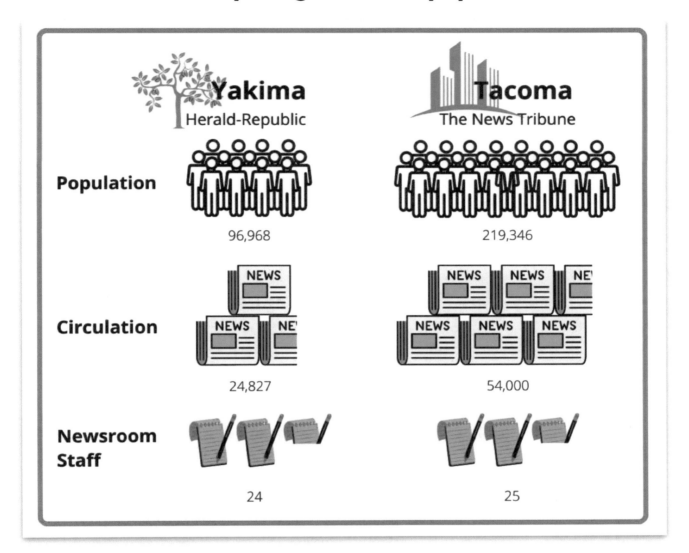

Figure 2.   Credit: Kelly McNabb, News Study Committee

A nationwide decline

Newsroom staffing has plummeted, with a national decline of 50%. (Figure 3)

Washington state newsrooms lost 67% of their workers from 2005 to 2020, according to U.S. Sen. Maria Cantwell's October 2020 report, "Local Journalism: America's Most Trusted News Source Threatened."[8]

That wasn't as severe as the losses in Rhode Island, New Mexico, New Hampshire, New Jersey and Minnesota, where declines topped 80%. But it was worse than those in Utah, New York, Georgia and the District of Columbia, where decreases were 20% to 30%.

The Seattle Times experienced two staff reductions in 2008. Early in the year, the paper had to cut $21 million, leading to 17 layoffs and 69 losses by attrition, according to a National Press Photographers

Association newsletter. In April, publisher Frank Blethen announced another round of layoffs and freezes – 200 losses with 45 or more in the newsroom. The paper needed to trim another $15 million. Blethen said, "We had hoped the expense reductions made at the beginning of the year would prevent the need for further downsizing. But that is not the case."[9]

Of course, the significant staff losses at The Seattle Times were nothing compared with what happened to Seattle's other daily, the Post-Intelligencer. The P-I ceased publishing a print edition the following year, eventually transitioning into a primarily online aggregator of information from other sources. More about the P-I is provided later in this report.

Pandemic impact

COVID-19 dealt a further blow to newsrooms across the country, including those in Washington. "Almost no paper in Washington has remained unscathed," Seattle Times business reporter Katherine Khashimova Long wrote in March 2020. The pandemic prompted widespread business closures and event cancellations, which then led to significant advertising losses. The reduced advertising revenue in turn

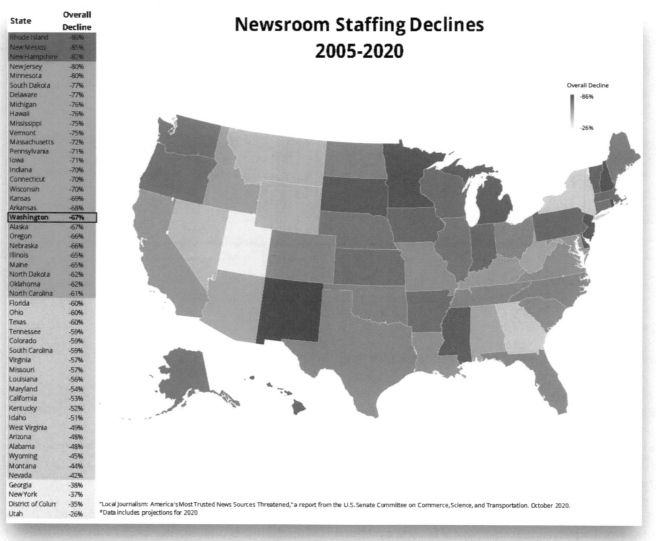

Figure 3

resulted in the need to cut jobs[10].

At Sound Publishing, which owned at least 40 publications at the time, management announced cuts to its 350-person staff. In one case, that left six part-time reporters in the Seattle area to produce content for 11 papers. Long quoted publisher Josh O'Connor as saying Sound Publishing had to temporarily shutter nine of 13 free community weeklies. Sound is an Everett-based firm that owns newspapers in Washington state and Alaska. Sound Publishing is owned by Black Press Media, a Canadian corporation that also owns newspapers in British Columbia and Alberta.

In an interview with the news study committee, O'Connor said the spring 2020 state lockdown forced The (Everett) Daily Herald, the company's flagship, to lay off a quarter of its staff. He said the company also had to suspend 20 weeklies, although it relaunched seven of them two years later.

Page count decreases

	2004	2020
THE NEWS TRIBUNE	100 pages | $1.50	36 pages | $3.00
DAILY RECORD — Built on Trust, Focused on Community	26 pages | $0.50	12 pages | $1.00
THE BELLINGHAM HERALD	66 pages | $1.50	28 pages | $3.00
THE SPOKESMAN-REVIEW	82 pages | $1.50	60 pages | $2.00

Figure 4: Committee members compared page counts for four Washington state daily newspapers in 2004 and 2020 as another measure of the decline. In all four instances, the numbers of Sunday-edition pages decreased significantly while prices increased.
Credit: Kelly McNabb, News Study Committee

The Seattle Times managed better when the pandemic hit, reassigning sports reporters to other coverage when teams canceled play, Long wrote. She quoted Alan Fisco, president of The Seattle Times Co., as saying the paper didn't have to lay off employees and wasn't planning to do so.

A simple fact is that covering local government is a labor-intensive task. Humans are needed for accountability journalism. "When we lose reporters at the rate we're losing them, democracy suffers as there simply is less news about local governments and that translates into less transparency in how our elected leaders carry out their responsibilities on behalf of the citizens who elected them," said researcher Marcus E. Howard.[11]

Fewer pages

Another way to look at the decline in local news is to consider the number of pages in a newspaper. Fewer pages reflect less coverage.

Aided by librarians at the Washington State Library and the Pacific Northwest Room of the Tacoma Public Library, the study committee tracked the number of pages in four newspapers on a Sunday and a Wednesday in three years – 2004, 2012 and 2020.

The News Tribune, The Bellingham Herald, the Daily Record in Ellensburg and The Spokesman-Review all had significant reductions in pages. All had price increases, too, with three papers doubling their rates. (Figure 4) The News Tribune had the most notable reduction, from 100 pages on a Sunday in 2004 to 36 pages in 2020.

The Bellingham Herald, meanwhile, saw page counts drop from 66 on a Sunday in 2004 to 28 in 2020. The price doubled to $3. The Daily Record in Ellensburg saw its page counts drop from 26 on a Sunday in 2004 to 12 in 2020. The price also doubled, from 50 cents to $1.

The Spokesman-Review, which launched a major drive to build community support and shift its focus to local news, cut the fewest pages. A Sunday paper in Spokane in 2004 numbered 82 pages but 60 in 2020. Per-copy prices went from $1.50 to $2. The Wednesday page counts dropped from 46 in 2004 to 28 in 2020.

Washington Daily Newspapers

Newspaper	City	Owner	Circulation	Increase/Decrease Since 2008
The Wenatchee World	Wenatchee	Wick Communications (World Publishing)	15,001	↓
Peninsula Daily News	Port Angeles	Sound Publishing	11,724	↓
The Columbian	Vancouver	Columbian Publishing Co	48,078	↓
The Daily News	Longview	Lee Enterprises	18,536	↓
Tri-City Herald	Kennewick	Chatham Asset Management	25,663	↓
Columbia Basin Herald	Moses Lake	Hagadone Corporation	7,780	↓
The Daily World	Aberdeen	Sound Publishing	6,281	↓
The Seattle Times	Seattle	Seattle Times Company	210,156	↓
Kitsap Sun	Kitsap	Gannett	16,683	↓
Daily Record	Ellensburg	Adams Publishing Group	5,523	Constant
The Chronicle	Centralia	CT Publishing	10,200	↓
The News Tribune	Tacoma	Chatham Asset Management	54,000	↓
Skagit Valley Herald	Mount Vernon	Adams Publishing Group	13,942	↓
The Daily Herald	Everett	Sound Publishing	33,543	↓
The Spokesman-Review	Spokane	Cowles Publishing Co	56,629	↓
The Olympian	Olympia	Chatham Asset Management	17,401	↓
Walla Walla Union-Bulletin	Walla Walla	Seattle Times Company	11,731	↓
The Bellingham Herald	Bellingham	Chatham Asset Management	13,073	↓
Cascadia Daily News	Bellingham	David Syre		New Jan. 2022
Yakima Herald-Republic	Yakima	Seattle Times Company	24,827	↓

*Data sourced 2022

Figure 5   Credit: News Study Committee

COVID-19 affected page counts as well. Chris Bennett, who publishes four newspapers and a radio station that serve the Black community, said the virus struck a hard blow to his publications, including The Seattle Medium. In the early 2000s, he said, The Medium published at least 16 pages each week. "During COVID, we were reaching the bare minimum of six pages. We have been fortunate enough to build that back up recently."

Newspaper closures

Much reporting on the decline of local news focuses on the number of newspapers that have closed. As previously noted, research indicates the United States lost 25% of its newspapers from 2004 to 2020. Washington state has lost 20%.[12]

Rowland Thompson, executive director of the trade association Allied Daily Newspapers of Washington, reminisced about some of the better days for the state's newspapers. "Seattle and Spokane had two daily newspapers until 10 and 25 years ago, respectively, and Bellevue had a daily newspaper and so did Kent until 15 years ago," Thompson told the study committee.

From 2004 through April 2022, the number of weekly newspapers in Washington dropped from 116 to 96, according to a number of sources, including the Washington Newspaper Publishers Association. Along with those 20 closures, a few new papers were launched, a few merged and at least one daily transitioned to a weekly.

Tallying the number of operating dailies is not as simple, largely because of differences over the definition of a daily. Some might consider a five-day-a-week business publication a daily, but others wouldn't if the paper didn't report regularly on local government and schools.

For example, the Seattle Daily Journal of Commerce, which the Washington Newspaper Publishers Association recognizes as a daily, and the Tacoma Daily Index don't provide regular coverage of local governance or broader civic issues.

Meanwhile, the Daily Record in Ellensburg, once a six-days-a-week paper, publishes a print edition four days a week and an online edition once a week. Similarly, the Yakima Herald-Republic, in a move many observers say foretells the future of newspapers, announced in early 2022 that it would cut back to printing three times a week while posting more frequently on its website.[13] But both of the latter papers feature some local news, including reporting on city and county government and schools, although the coverage at the Daily Record is not comprehensive.

This study follows guidance from The Associated Press, which considers a paper a daily if it provides original local news reporting three or more days a week. We count 20 dailies in Washington as of April 2022. Except for the Cascadia Daily News in Bellingham, which launched in January 2022, all of the daily papers listed were publishing in 2004. Plus, there was the Daily Sun-News in Yakima, which was replaced by the weekly Sunnyside Sun in 2018. (Figure 5)

Washington also had three more print dailies: the Seattle Post-Intelligencer, the King County Journal and the Kent Reporter. Sound Publishing bought The Kent Reporter and publishes it now as a weekly. Sound also bought the Journal in November 2006, but closed it two months later.

Over the years, the Post-Intelligencer won two Pulitzer Prizes for editorial cartooning and could count among its bylines those of E.B. White, Frank Herbert and Tom Robbins. It ceased publishing a print edition in 2009 and today is strictly an online publication that mostly aggregates content from other publications.

While this study distinguishes between dailies and weeklies as newspapers themselves do, it should be noted that the digital world has lessened that distinction somewhat. That is because a number of weeklies update their online web sites with breaking news. In Portland, Oregon, for instance, the (weekly) Willamette Week earned a Pulitzer Prize in 2005 for a story it published online a few days before the story appeared in print.

Suburban coverage

The weeklies that closed between 2004 and 2022 once served busy suburbs of Seattle, Tacoma and Everett and rural regions, including the counties of Adams, Ferry, Grant, Grays Harbor and Yakima. Some might wonder if the dailies filled in the coverage lost by the closure of those weeklies. But observers said all of the remaining dailies have lost significant staff and advertising, causing them to rein in their own primary coverage.

Thompson, of the Allied Daily Newspapers of Washington, said the closures of weeklies and the reduction of coverage by daily newspapers has hit heavily populated regions. Sizable suburban communities no longer have newspapers paying close attention to the actions of their city councils and school boards, he said.

In King County, while three new weekly papers opened, 11 papers closed between 2004 and 2022. One daily also transitioned into a weekly. In Snohomish County, nine publications shuttered while two opened.

Mike Fancher was the executive editor of The Seattle Times until his retirement in 2008. He explained how the coverage of suburban Seattle transformed. In the mid-1970s, Fancher wrote, the paper began to build a robust operation with three bureaus to report on the bedroom communities: Eastside, South Snohomish County and North Pierce County. In the early 2000s, at their zenith, each bureau had an office staffed by an editor and at least six reporters who covered education, government and high school sports. "High school sports was a big draw for suburban readers," he said.

The Times' local news section, Fancher said, included a page devoted to the suburbs with readers in each area receiving news specific to their communities. "Competition was fierce," he said. Though the Post-Intelligencer didn't focus much on the suburbs, The Daily Herald published a separate edition covering South Snohomish County and the Journal-American in Bellevue, which later became the King County Journal, competed with a full staff on the east side. The News Tribune covered north Pierce County.

Washington has lost more than 20 newspapers since 2004, although the state has seen the launch of a few new publications. The Seattle Post-Intelligencer stopped publishing a print edition in 2009 and now is an online publication. Credit: camknows. (CC BY-NC-SA 2.0)

But following a Newspaper Guild strike in 2001 at the two Seattle dailies, the Times began to cut staff, followed by the big cuts that came with the 2008 recession. "The suburban bureaus closed shortly after that," Fancher said.

Rural communities

Northwest of Seattle, the residents of Island County could choose to subscribe to the Times. But the Times coverage of Oak Harbor, Langley and Coupeville is predominantly limited to reporting on Navy jet noise concerns, features, weather and the region as a travel destination.

Sound Publishing promotes its Island County papers as the local source for information for the 80,000 residents. According to Sound Publishing's website, print circulation of the Whidbey News-Times is 3,116 while the South Whidbey Record's is 2,374 and the Whidbey Crosswind, which serves the military community, is 6,138.

Another way to gauge the decline is to tally counties where no newspaper is published. Northwestern University researcher Penelope Abernathy calls that a news desert.

Jacob Grumbach

More than 200 of the country's 3,143 counties published no newspaper of their own in 2020, Abernathy reported. She identified Washington as among the states having one county without a paper of its own. Oregon and California each have two counties with no newspapers and Alaska has 13 counties without a newspaper, the third worst in the nation. Georgia tops the list with 28 no-newspaper counties.

Because no newspaper is published in southeastern Washington's Asotin County (population 22,480), Abernathy identifies it as a news desert.

Technically, that is correct. However, Asotin is served by The Lewiston Tribune just across the border in Idaho, said city editor Matt Baney. "We have a person who regularly covers Asotin County, including county and city government," Baney said. "Our staff also covers schools, sports and outdoor events." He said about a third of the Tribune's subscribers live in Asotin County.

The difficulty of that task is described by Jacob Grumbach, assistant professor of political science at the University of Washington. "In southeast Washington, they share a border with Idaho, and the Lewiston Tribune is attempting to cover the valley between two states and two legislatures, surrounded by agricultural land, with little tiny towns that all have town councils," he said.

Either way, portions of Washington, particularly rural areas in the center and east, have papers with low circulations, even considering their populations.

In Pend Oreille County, where the population is 13,724, subscribers to the Newport Miner number 1,700. Following the 2021 closure of the weekly Othello Outlook, Adams County,

News Deshorts: The Demographics		
Demographic Measure	News Deserts	U.S.
Average Poverty Rate	16%	11%
Average Median Annual Income	$51,942	$67,521
Average Median Age (Years)	43	38
Average Percent of Residents with Bachelor's Degree or Higher	20%	38%

Figure 6   Medill Local News Initiative, Local News Initiative Database and US Census Bureau

with a population of 20,274, has the weekly Ritzville Adams County Journal, with a circulation of about 2,146. In the northeast, the 2016 closure of the weekly Republic News Miner left only the weekly Ferry County View, which has a circulation of 1,250, to serve that county's 7,594 residents.

Rob Curley, of The Spokesman-Review, said six counties around Spokane County are in essence news deserts even though they have some small newspapers. The editor said he provided that information when he applied for – and received – a grant from Report for America to hire a reporter to cover rural areas in Eastern Washington. One of the first positions for which the Spokane paper received financing from Report for America was in 2019. It was for a rural health reporter.

**Penelope Muse
Abernathy**

Researcher Penelope Abernathy, in her 2022 study, provided data about the demographics of a news desert. She compared U.S. counties overall with U.S. counties that she identified as news deserts.

News deserts, she reported, have a 16% average poverty rate, compared with 11% for others; the average median annual income in a news desert county is $51,942 compared with $67,521; the average age of a resident in a news desert is 43 years compared with 38 years; and 20% of residents in a news desert county hold at least a four-year college degree, while that number is 38% otherwise.[14] (Figure 6)

See A Deeper Dive for Cascadia Daily News comes to town
See A Deeper Dive for Washington newspapers 2004 vs. 2002, a comprehensive list
See A Deeper Dive for Newspapers by County, a comprehensive list and map
See A Deeper Dive for Newspapers by Sound Publishing

U.S counties without a newspaper

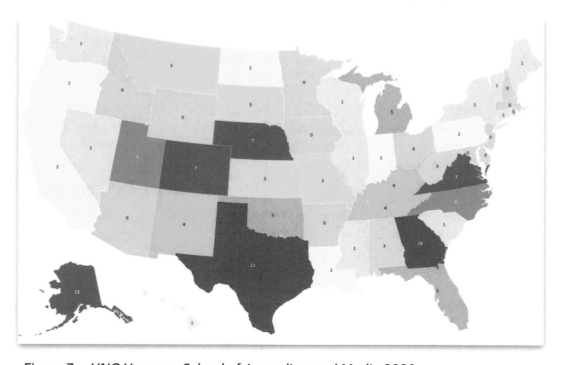

Figure 7   UNC Hussman School of Journalism and Media 2020

Ethnic newspapers

Ethnic newspapers are those that produce news stories and other content for a particular cultural or linguistic group or ethnic community, according to the Seattle Office of Immigrant and Refugee Affairs. These publications have faced declining interest in newspapers as well. Here's a look at how some have dealt with the challenges.

The Seattle Medium

Chris Bennett vividly recalls the day early in the pandemic when an elderly woman made her way into the newsroom of The Seattle Medium, the newspaper he owns that serves the city's Black community. As was her routine, the woman had taken a bus to her hair salon to pick up a copy of the latest edition of the weekly.

But with COVID-19 on the rise, the salon was shuttered. Determined to get her paper, she took another bus, this one to her church. But the pandemic had closed the church, too. She boarded a third bus to a store. But the store was closed as well.

"She made her way to our office to see if we had some papers," Bennett said. "She did this all on the bus."

Such reader loyalty has helped papers serving communities of color weather the local news crisis, their publishers say. "It's the inroads and connections we've had in the community over the years," Bennett told the study committee. "We don't just produce news and information. We're actually kind of a focal point."

Chris Bennett

Bennett's family-owned company, Tiloben Publishing, in business in the Pacific Northwest since 1970, also publishes the Seattle Metro Homemaker shoppers guide, the Tacoma True Citizen, and The Portland Medium. The company owns two Seattle radio stations and one in Portland, too. Bennett said the company's mission is straightforward: to help improve the quality of life of Blacks and underserved communities.

"We cover a mix of topics," including local government, culture, and politics, Bennett said. "If it impacts the community or affects the quality of life of African-Americans, we cover it."

Circulation has remained steady at 13,500, despite the pandemic and the decline of advertising. But the page count has fluctuated greatly, dropping from 16 to six pages at times. "It's a struggle because it's all based on advertising," Bennett explained. When COVID-19 hit, advertisers canceled their orders. Staffing has been affected, too.

"We're trying to build back … because there are so many stories we need to tell. That is a struggle. It's a balancing act." Community support for the paper, which grew during the Black Lives Matter movement and following George Floyd's death, has not diminished during the pandemic, Bennett said. "There is a real sense of people wanting to be engaged and wanting to be involved, wanting to make a difference."

The publishing company has responded by sponsoring scholarships, organizing food, clothing and relief drives, and other civic efforts. Like mainstream papers throughout the state, The Medium has sought support from other entities. Google's News Initiative program provides guidance to Medium staff members who are developing the paper's digital side. And the paper also has joined the Local Media Association for help with community fundraising.

The Black Lens

Across the state, Sandy Williams publishes The Black Lens, a monthly publication serving Spokane's Black community. The Black Lens was born in January 2015 after Williams picked up a copy of The Spokesman-Review and read about a state study on racial bias and the use of force by area law enforcement. Williams wasn't convinced of the veracity of what she read – that no bias existed – and got her own copy of the report.

Williams said she learned that law enforcement had used force 10 times more often against people of color. "I decided I would write that article and that's when it became a newspaper," she said.

Williams takes no salary; her mother and volunteers help with distribution. The Black Lens website serves as a repository for past editions. Williams said the paper serves a need in the African-American community. "The Black community was struggling to address issues and connect with each other," she said. The paper has 500 paid subscriptions and delivers up to 1,300 copies.

Williams said the pandemic didn't affect the paper negatively. In fact, some readers, concerned the paper might close, increased their support. "I'd be at some community event, and people would press a $50 bill in my hand. They were afraid The Black Lens would go away," she said.

Sandy Williams

She's been sensitive that the pandemic has impacted others, opting not to charge advertisers who encountered tough times. "I know the community and I know who is struggling," she said.

Like at The Medium, Williams said community support increased dramatically in the wake of George Floyd's death and the growth of the Black Lives Matter movement.

In fact, the January 2022 issue was the paper's largest with 40 pages. But it is also the last edition for at least a year. Williams also directs a nonprofit community organization in Spokane and explained she needs to take a yearlong hiatus from the paper to focus on building a community center.

After this report was written, Williams, 60, died in a seaplane crash in Puget Sound over Labor Day weekend 2022, one of 10 victims in the crash.

South Seattle Emerald

"Amplifying the authentic narratives of South Seattle" is the mission of the South Seattle Emerald, a Black-led online publication that identifies as a hyperlocal serving Seattle and suburban communities from Burien to the east and from Tukwila south to Kent. Founded in 2014, the publication purchases content from some 40 freelancers each month with wide-ranging coverage. Recent articles dealt with the monkeypox outbreak in the Pacific Northwest, an all-BIPOC burlesque festival, primary candidates for the 37th Legislative District, and summer community events.

Emerald leadership reported the paper enjoyed its most profitable year in 2020, collecting funds from donations and grants for specific topics and projects. A fundraiser to celebrate the paper's seventh anniversary that year collected more than $8,000 over its $50,000 target.

According to the publication, online views increased by 500% that year to 200,000 views per month. It boasts of more than 36,000 followers on social media and nearly 2,000 subscribers to its weekly newsletter.

News in Spanish at El Sol de Yakima

Gloria Ibañez

Gloria Ibañez has been with El Sol de Yakima since 2004. She was hired as a full-time news reporter, joining a staff that included a copy editor and a news editor.

Today, Ibañez is the only full-time staffer. Besides reporting and writing, she now edits. Two freelancers report, one from California and the other from Seattle. Page design is handled by staff from El Sol's parent company, the Yakima Herald-Republic, where Ibañez has her office.

The Herald-Republic's parent company, The Seattle Times Co., provides support, too. "The company wants to keep El Sol de Yakima. The paper is very important for the community," Ibañez said.

She translates stories produced by Herald-Republic and Times staff members, and publishes them in El Sol. "We publish sports news from the Seahawks and the Sounders and business news. They need to know all of this because we are part of the community," she said.

A free paper, El Sol reported a circulation of 17,100 in 2021, its highest to date. Ibañez said the paper's focus is on local news, particularly since the pandemic. Spanish-language television news provides national news coverage, "but we need to inform our people who live here."

The importance of meaningful local news became particularly clear during the pandemic. County health officials conducted all of their news conferences in English at first. Ibañez told officials that translating their information into Spanish, including video reports, was time consuming, and particularly problematic without any staff. County officials responded and since have provided information in Spanish as well.

The paper also has received funding to assist with translation, including grants from the Valley Community Foundation and Group Health. Ibañez noted Yakima County is 51% Hispanic. "Some of the people here are bilingual, speaking both English and Spanish. Some of them are only Spanish speaking," she said.

News for Native Americans

Journalist Betty Oppenheimer previously reported for the Sequim Gazette and is now communications specialist for the Jamestown S'Klallam tribe. Coverage of Native American communities and issues is not extensive in mainstream newspapers, limited to environmental conflicts and controversies concerning casinos and the gaming industry, she said. Oppenheimer mails a monthly newsletter to a distribution list of about 700, and sends press releases about tribal news to local newspapers. The newsletter is funded by the tribe and is distributed free of charge.

"I'm an advocate journalist, so I always write the tribe's perspective. It's important for people to understand what's available to them, and whether they need to be tribal or not tribal to access these services.

"We're fortunate here on the Olympic Peninsula because we have three weeklies and one daily paper. They were locally owned, and now they're owned by a conglomerate but they're still written by local folks. I will say that their staffing has really shrunk, so they work with me a lot," Oppenheimer said.

Betty Oppenheimer

"I think people are getting out of the habit or maybe never got into the habit of reading a paper," Oppenheimer said. "I think the decline and availability has caused a decline in people expecting that information to be available and looking for it."

Three Northwest newspapers – The News Tribune in Tacoma, The Olympian and The Bellingham Herald – partnered with Report for America to hire Natasha Brennan for two years to cover Indigenous affairs.[15]

Among Brennan's recent reporting were stories about a Department of Interior allocation of $46 million to tribes to address climate change, a grant to support Indigenous artists and Earth Day celebrations in Bellingham.

Tammy Ayer

Meanwhile in Yakima, the Herald-Republic has produced extensive reporting on the murder and disappearance of dozens of Indigenous women. A collection of stories by reporter Tammy Ayer about the fate of dozens of Yakama Nation women has raised awareness of the tragedy locally, statewide and nationally.

Executive editor Greg Halling said Ayer began writing about the issue in 2018. "Her work has had tremendous impact and what you see now is that people are now willing to step forward and share their stories. Her work has convinced a big part of Washington that this topic deserves our attention."

Ayer's stories are presented on a site titled The Vanished that also includes case histories and resources.[16]

See A Deeper Dive for Publications serving ethnic communities in Washington state

Who let the watchdogs out?

Former Associated Press state news editor Paul Queary remembers the scene in the two press office buildings near the Capitol in Olympia two decades ago. The buildings "were packed to the rafters. If you had interns – and pretty much everyone did – they were lucky if they had desks," Queary wrote in a 2021 issue of Post Alley.[17]

"The concentration of journalists drew politicians, flacks and the few lobbyists who didn't view the press with fear, loathing, or both. Impromptu visits from newsmakers ranging from Tim Eyman to U.S. Sen. Patty Murray weren't uncommon," Queary wrote.

Covering the Capitol full time in Olympia, he explained, were three reporters from The Seattle Times, three from AP, two from The Olympian, one from the Seattle Post-Intelligencer, and one from The News Tribune. Additionally, there were reporters from The Spokesman-Review, the Tri-City Herald, The (Vancouver) Columbian, The (Longview) Daily News, The (Everett) Daily Herald and The Bellingham Herald, some of whom who were in Olympia only during legislative sessions.

That's at least 16 full- and part-timers.

Today, five journalists are assigned full time by their respective outlets to report on the doings of the governor, 49 senators and 98 representatives, and the hundreds of employees who work in scores of agencies. (See Figure 8) News outlets have become creative in dealing with this situation during the legislative session. The Washington Newspaper Publishers Association, for one, sponsors internships for college students who work on site with WNPA editors. The reporting by these interns is shared with association member newspapers, many which are weeklies and unable to send reporters.

Nonetheless, the depletion of the Olympia news bureau means "in-depth and accountability reporting" is gone, Queary said. Most beat coverage is gone, too, with all of the reporters writing about the same big story of the day. There is much less oversight of elected officials.

For 37 years, David Ammons covered state government for the AP. He left in 2008 to become the communications director for the Washington Secretary of State's office. In 2017, Gov. Jay Inslee appointed him to the state Public Disclosure Commission, which he later chaired.

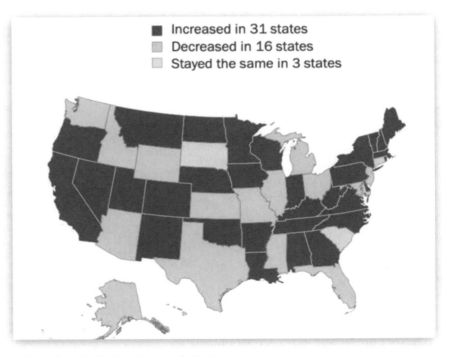

Washington statehouse reporters reduced by half

■ Increased in 31 states
▨ Decreased in 16 states
□ Stayed the same in 3 states

Figure 8   **Credit: Pew Research Center**

Ammons told the news study committee that the depletion has left a troubling imbalance. "Legislators and staff have more power than ever," he said. "I think probably if the truth be told, the Legislature likes not being watched as closely," he said. "Legislators will have their flacks tweet and send out information on their bills from their points of view and how they are saving the world."

In Washington, D.C., U.S. Rep. Derek Kilmer represents the state's 6th Congressional District. "I think it's important for elected officials to be accountable to the people that they represent," Kilmer told the news study committee, "having a local press to serve that watchdog role."

David Ammons

Kilmer served in the state Legislature from 2005 to 2012. He recalled the persistence of Joe Turner, a News Tribune reporter. "He looked under every rock for issues when the new Narrows Bridge was getting built and tried to find every angle in which people were getting screwed and that was really important."

Kilmer also recalled the years when journalists in Olympia covered stories with an eye on what their readers needed. "There was a pretty healthy Capitol press corps that was always sort of focused on the issues that mattered to their local community," he said. At times, Kilmer said, those journalists brought to light problems the lawmakers themselves were unaware of: "Sometimes they would run articles on a subject and you'd say, 'Gosh! I didn't know that problem existed. So, let's go to work on that.'"

Today, though, the reduced staffing means reporters have to chase "the story of the day," meaning they are unable to tailor stories to address readers' needs as much as they might like, said Jonathan Brunt, political and government editor of The Spokesman-Review. The Spokesman-Review is fortunate to have a full-time reporter in Olympia to focus on issues of significance to Spokane readers, Brunt said. But readers in Yakima and other eastside communities suffer because there are no other newspapers east of the Cascades with a full-time Olympia presence, he said.

True, The Seattle Times, which owns the Herald-Republic, has a full-time reporter in Olympia. But because Seattle is so much larger than Yakima, the Times' Capitol bureau reporter has to focus more on stories important to readers in that area, Brunt said.

Reporters fill the hall for a press conference called by Gov. Booth Gardner, whose back is to the camera. Gardner served from 1985 to 1993, when the Capitol bureau was more robust than today.
Credit: Legislative Support Services.

A similar scenario plays out for small papers that rely on the AP for their Olympia coverage, said Jim Camden, a

Karen Keiser

semi-retired Spokesman-Review columnist and retired Olympia bureau chief. "Small papers relying on pool coverage … aren't going to get coverage tailored for the small towns," he said. Camden said that's the case, too, for the Tri-City Herald. Its sister paper, The News Tribune, has a full-time Olympia reporter. But again, with Tacoma's population exceeding that of the Tri-Cities, The News Tribune reporter has to focus on what Tacoma readers need.

Meanwhile, state Sen. Karen Keiser, D-Des Moines, describes today's news industry as being in a "real jam." A former television journalist who earned a master's degree in journalism from the University of California, Berkeley, Keiser said she believes the decline has left people uninformed. "Voters are not empowered if they … are not getting information from reliable sources," she said.

Additionally, the lack of coverage means many people don't understand the workings of government or how to interact with government agencies, she said. Keiser said she and many of her colleagues send newsletters to keep constituents informed, as Ammons mentioned. She acknowledged the newsletters don't necessarily feature the unbiased reporting that a responsible local news organization would provide.

Politics and government aren't covered only in Olympia, of course.

Queary said the decline in reporters has resulted in limited coverage of city councils, county councils, school boards, special district boards and county boards of commissioners throughout the state. This can also impact local issues, like discipline of police officers. Queary speculated that a particular incident might have played out differently in Kent had the local news environment been healthier.

> "I think probably if the truth be told, the Legislature likes not being watched as closely."
> — David Ammons

According to Query, there was no coverage of a 2019 complaint against a deputy police chief who, an investigation the following year revealed, had posted a Nazi insignia on his office door and taken other questionable actions. The deputy chief was disciplined, but it wasn't until after an advocacy group filed a public-records request that the matter became public. After that, the mayor's office pursued the deputy chief's resignation. Queary posited that voters might not have returned the incumbent mayor to office had they known of the deputy chief's actions. He said he believes the King County Journal would have reported the story, but Sound Publishing purchased the paper in 2006 and closed it within four months.

Keiser noted similar problems in her district. The 39th Legislative District, which she represents, includes the communities of Kent, SeaTac, Burien and Des Moines, which have several blogs but no daily newspapers. "Weekly area newspapers don't provide sufficient coverage of local government," she said. "We have no oversight on our city council."

In some communities, non-journalists have taken matters into their own hands. In early 2022, Chris Randels, who describes himself as a community advocate, said he began live tweeting Bellevue City Council and transportation commission meetings. "It came out of necessity," he said. "I never really had imagined myself as a journalist per se. And then it just kind of slowly morphed in over time."[18]

Randels was speaking on KUOW radio's Soundside show and Libby Denkman, the show's moderator, said his efforts could be considered journalism. "He's bringing information to the public, not particularly because he wanted to, but because he saw a hole and wanted to fill it," she said.

Of course, as accurate and unbiased as they may be, Twitter reports by well-intentioned individuals attending local government meetings don't necessarily face the same scrutiny for objectivity and completeness as local newspaper reports that are assigned and reviewed by an editor.

More organized citizen efforts to inform the public take place elsewhere, such as in Okanogan County, where the Okanogan County Watch website features notes and reports about local agencies and meetings compiled by a team of volunteers. In May 2018, the Okanogan County Watch was recognized by the Washington Coalition for Open Government for its advocacy efforts on behalf of open government in the region.[19]

Alan Fisco

Another small weekly, the Chinook Observer, consistently tracks the goings on of local government, providing its 5,000 subscribers with solid coverage and hard news. The Observer has won awards for its reporting on heavy-handed immigration officials.

Meanwhile, The Seattle Times' Fisco said the company has taken a financial loss to keep the Yakima Herald-Republic's staff numbers from slipping further. Ten years ago, about 40 staff members worked in the newsroom. "Today, we have 24 newsroom employees," Fisco wrote in a December 2021 article in the Yakima paper. "Frankly, that is not enough to really serve you."[20]

See A Deeper Dive for Observer offers meaty coverage.

Causes

"Expensive, boring and wrong" is the snappy title of a 2021 article on the Nieman Lab website featuring reasons readers gave for canceling their news subscriptions.

Responses to the Nieman Lab survey ran the gamut: the subscription was too costly, no time to spare, inconsistent delivery, the publication is too conservative, it's too liberal, I didn't need the content, and the information wasn't trustworthy.[21]

From former subscribers of three longtime Washington state dailies came these explanations:

"Paper stopped covering city council and county commission meetings and, when asked, said no one read those stories and replaced with features and columns, many of which were written by readers/ businesses/ amateurs."
– The Spokesman-Review

"I used to work there, and the paper didn't cover the employees' subscriptions. When I quit my job, I canceled the subscriptions."
– The Seattle Times

"It was almost $20/month and it still showed me ads when I wanted to read the paper online. It made me log in again every time I wanted to read an article. The Report for America reporter was the only one reporting anything of substance."
– The Olympian

An accompanying story reported nearly a third of the 500 respondents said money was the main reason they canceled. Another 30% identified "ideology" or "politics," and 13% had other reasons, including content that was not useful. Customer service and too little time were mentioned, too.[22]

Obviously, news publications aren't keeping all readers happy.

Internet and social media impact on newspapers

The internet and social media play major roles in the story of the decline of local news. Clear indications of their role became apparent in 2008, at the beginning of the Great Recession. That year, online news platforms overtook print sources for people reading national and international news, according to a Pew Research Center report. (Figure 10)

Forty percent of people surveyed got "most of their news about national and international issues from the internet." That was up from 24% in 2007. By the following year, the majority of younger audiences – those less than 30 years old – already preferred online sources for national and international news with nearly six in 10 respondents turning there. (Figure 9)

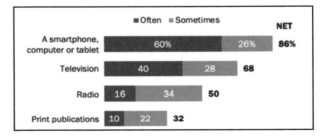

Most Americans get news on digital devices

Figure 9.   Pew Research Center, survey of U.S. adults conducted Aug. 31 to Sept 7, 2020

Within a decade, 34% of all Americans Pew surveyed were going online – to news websites or social media – for all of their news, although television remained the most popular news source at 41%.[23]

Since then, the digital attraction has continued to grow. By 2021, Pew reported more than 80% of Americans surveyed got their news from a smartphone, computer or tablet "often" or "sometimes."[24] (Figure 10) About a third said they got their news from print publications "at least sometimes" with only 10% turning to print "often."

Observers have blamed the newspapers for slowly responding to technological advances and improvements. Observers say local newspaper outlets were particularly slow to accommodate the personal habits of more technology-savvy audiences, including younger people, who turn to phone apps for everything from shopping to budgeting.

Some papers were initially reluctant to embrace online format because they feared financial repercussions, said Benjamin Shors, the Washington State University professor. "Many of those papers decided if we go online, we risk our print publications. And so, we're not going to go into that online space."

The assumption that advertisers would prefer less expensive online ads over print turned out to be true. "For every $1 increase in online advertising between 2005 and 2011, newspapers lost $22 in print advertising," two academic researchers reported.[25]

Newspapers also were slow to move their content behind paywalls because they feared readers would not be willing to pay for news that previously was free. In 2009, only 5% of survey respondents said they were willing to pay for online news from their favored news purveyor, while 75% said they'd look for a news source that did not charge.[26]

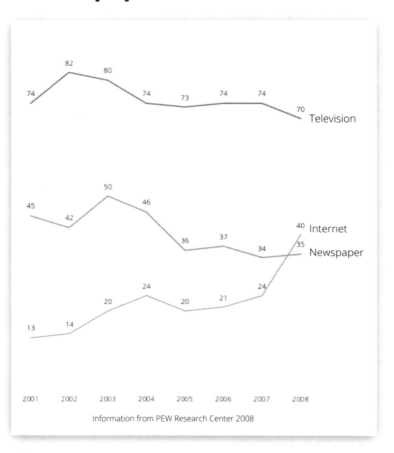

Internet surpassed newspapers as news source

Information from PEW Research Center 2008

Figure 10

In the early years, the internet was still a bit of an unknown, and not all people were convinced of its viability. In 1995, Newsweek's Clifford Stoll predicted that the internet would turn out to be a passing fancy. "The truth is no online database will replace your daily newspaper," the technology writer said.[27]

The shift to online advertising

The primary source of newspaper revenue had been from advertisers. Decline of print advertising dollars has been pivotal in shrinking and shutting local papers. (Figures 11 and 12) Prior to 2000, considered the heyday of local newspapers, many "operated at an 80-20 split, meaning 80% of a paper's revenue was coming from advertising and 20 was coming from circulation (subscriptions)," said The Spokesman-Review's Curley.

But as advertisers have found online platforms less expensive than print and with more targeted distribution, they shifted their purchases. Today, Curley said, 35% of The Spokesman-Review's revenue is from advertising and 65% comes from subscriptions, which doesn't generate sufficient operating funds. That scenario has been playing out across the country. A Pew Research Center 2021 study reported advertising revenue had dropped a full one-quarter from 2019.[28]

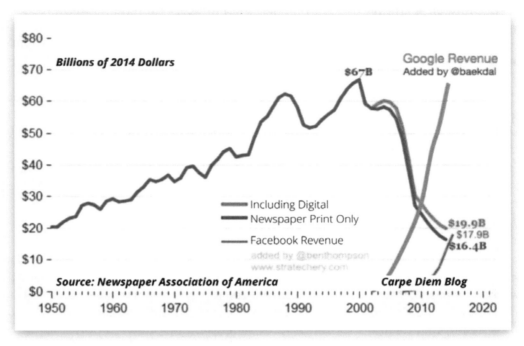

Figure 11   Source: Newspaper Association of America, revised by @benthompson and @baekdal

Newspapers have attracted digital advertisers, but shifting formats have also brought new costs to build and maintain websites and mobile applications. According to Pew, digital advertising accounted for 39% of newspaper advertising revenue in 2020, up from 35% in the previous year.[29]

One can easily understand why many advertisers prefer digital, whether on the newspaper's online content or through third-party news amalgamators like Facebook. Consider these figures Sen. Maria Cantwell's report provided on costs for advertisers in 2015 to reach 400,000 people:

- Los Angeles Times print: $40,000.
- Los Angeles Times digital: $5,600.
- Google Search: $16.

The shift of advertising from newspapers to amalgamators including Google, Facebook, and others, coincided with explosive growth of these "big tech" firms. Industry observers, including The Seattle Times' Fisco, blame Big Tech giants for sizable advertising losses. They point to the profits Facebook and Google make from advertising they sell that accompanies news stories produced by the newspaper outlets without remunerating the newspapers for their content.

At the Yakima Herald-Republic, which The Times owns, Fisco blamed the rise of Big Tech for a "decimation" of the paper's advertising revenue. Fisco said the Herald-Republic saw ad revenue decrease 30% during the pandemic. Since 2015, it has fallen 60%.

Sen. Cantwell is among the tech giants' chief critics. When her Commerce Committee released a major report on the news industry in October 2020, she said, "Local news has been hijacked by a few large news aggregation platforms." She pointed expressly to Google and Facebook, calling them "the dominant players in online advertising."[30]

The report said Google posts headlines and portions of stories it doesn't produce while Facebook posts content by publishers and users. The tech companies collect revenues in the billions from ads that run next to news reports that others produce, Cantwell and others assert.

Google and Facebook have acknowledged the tremendous pressure facing local news, but argue that posting stories for readers, who are often redirected to the publisher's site, serves the publisher's interest.

A changing marketplace

A number of observers said a changing marketplace that has seen greater consolidation among retailers is another factor in the advertising decline. Previously, Fisco wrote, local drug stores, markets and other retailers, including car dealers and furniture stores, bought individual advertising in local papers. But many of the large conglomerates that have acquired local retailers now pursue other advertising options. "As a result, Yakima and thousands of other community newspapers struggle for survival," he said.

Fisco said leadership at the Yakima paper has responded responsibly, cutting expenses by more than $6 million over four years. But those cuts haven't been enough. Fisco said the Yakima paper had been close to break-even financially. "Now, over the past two years, our losses will exceed $1 million."

Gayl Curtiss, who retired as general manager at the Hacker Group, one of Seattle's largest advertising agencies, painted an equally dire picture of the impact of the internet and social media on newspapers and her industry. "It was like a fire coming out of a hose, not a ripple, but a roar. It was disruptive," she said.

Curtiss, in the field for 30 years, said social media advertising may not be of the same quality as print, but it's faster as well as cheaper. With print, Curtiss explained, "You take time to come up with the campaign, with the ads. With the internet, you have to come up with something new the next day."

In time, Curtiss said, "Speed became more important than quality. This gutted the advertising world." The rapid turnover of digital content appeals to younger people, which furthers the print decline among a growing audience, she added. "Younger people … use apps, and shop by the internet. The newspaper is seen as old news. The internet is the primary source of news for many people. Every day that passes, newspapers become less relevant."

The former advertising executive also noted two of the most popular newspaper features used to be obituaries and classified ads. But now mortuaries run obituaries online and classifieds appear on Facebook and Craigslist. "There are more people on Community Connect (Facebook) than there are Daily Record subscribers in Kittitas County," Curtiss said.

At The Seattle Medium, publisher Chris Bennett said Craigslist, which made selling everything from a used car to baseball cards as easy as a few computer keystrokes, dramatically reduced classified ad sales to daily newspapers. "Classified advertising was your cash cow, for it financed everything," Bennett said. "Back in the day, pages of classifieds would finance your entertainment news pages, your sports pages, your business news pages, and your home and garden pages. But all these pages went when classifieds dried up."

See A Deeper Dive to learn about Craigslist, the "newspaper killer"

Some of the challenges for newspapers stemmed from the Great Recession of 2008-2009, the economic catastrophe that caused millions of people to lose their jobs and homes.

Newspapers experienced another financially tough year in 2015, severe enough that the Pew Research Center reported that year might as well have been a recession year for newspapers. Circulation — print and digital — fell 7% that year and advertising fell 8%. Particularly worrisome was that the advertising decrease in 2015 was on top of a 15% decrease in 2008 and a 27% decrease in 2009.[31] [32] Circulation refers to both subscription and newsstands sales.

Fisco said news outlets that own their presses can benefit from commercial printing work for other publications and non-newspaper clients. But as economic times have worsened, news outlets are seeing that option slip away. That's what happened at the Yakima Herald-Republic. Tough times forced the Herald-Republic to sell its building in 2021, which meant it had to shutter its commercial printing operation.

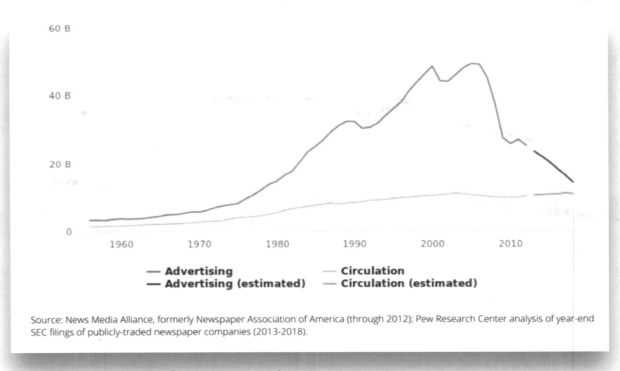

Advertising and circulation revenue

Source: News Media Alliance, formerly Newspaper Association of America (through 2012); Pew Research Center analysis of year-end SEC filings of publicly-traded newspaper companies (2013-2018).

Figure 12   *Revenue for newspaper industry*

Shift from local to national news

There are other theories about reasons for the local news decline.

Three university economists trace the start of the decline to the arrival of television in the late 1940s. Television prompted newspapers to reduce local coverage, which has led to a series of transformations and new trends, including more partisan voting patterns.[33]

Curley, The Spokesman-Review editor, traces the decline to Watergate in the early 1970s. "At that moment, the front pages of newspapers across America began to change," he said. Editors and publishers at local papers were more focused on impressing readers and other journalists and began to mimic the papers that were breaking one of the biggest stories in modern history. "It was the rise of a national paper that we hadn't seen before, like a USA Today," he said.

But Curley and others said that pursuing a national focus misses the mark. Local newspapers succeed when they provide news readers can use: information about schools, city and county councils, and local sports teams. Otherwise, people turn away.

David Zeeck, the former publisher of The News Tribune, said he saw that to be true when he joined the staff in 1994. Not long after he moved to Tacoma from the Kansas City Star, The News Tribune's publisher hired a media consultant. "She told me to do several things: emphasize sports, emphasize business, emphasize features, and cover the heck out of local news. We established the Statehouse bureau and a bureau in South King County," he explained.

Hedge fund takeovers

From television to digital to radio to print, the news is about the increasing number of purchases of local and regional news outlets by hedge funds. These purchases have become so common that hedge funds now control half of U.S. daily newspapers. Hedge fund Alden Capital has been in the forefront of this effort, having purchased the storied Chicago Tribune, the Baltimore Sun, the New York Daily News and other papers in May 2021. When it comes to producing meaningful local content, hedge funds just don't perform.[34]

In fact, the common practice of companies like Alden Capital is to buy floundering local papers, lay off staff, sell the buildings that once housed bustling newsrooms, and operate the papers out of a central hub.[35]

Alden's practice is a reason The Washington Post's former media columnist Margaret Sullivan referred to the firm as "one of the most ruthless of the corporate strip-miners seemingly intent on destroying local journalism."[36] While investors win, others lose, and not only the reporters, editors, designers and photographers whose jobs are eliminated.

Nieman Lab reported in a March 2022 study that after hedge funds purchased 31 newspapers, staff and coverage promptly declined. "What was shocking to me is that all the acquisitions led to staffing changes almost immediately and an almost immediate drop in content," wrote lead author Benjamin LeBrun of McGill University.[37]

Since Chatham Asset Management's purchase of six Washington state newspapers from McClatchy in a 2020 bankruptcy sale, all have experienced significant reductions in staff and local content. [38] The papers are Tri-City Herald, The News Tribune, The Peninsula Gateway, Puyallup Herald, The Olympian, and the Bellingham Herald. Chatham owns 30 dailies across the country, and newspapers in Canada, as well.

In Tacoma, The News Tribune has a circulation of 54,000 but only one more news staffer than the Yakima Herald-Republic, with a circulation of 15,000. Fred Obee, executive director of the Washington Newspaper Publishers Association, wasn't delicate describing three of the papers Chatham purchased from McClatchy. "The Tacoma News Tribune, The Bellingham Herald and The Olympian are shadows of their former selves," he said.

Halling, the Yakima editor, meanwhile labeled both The Olympian and The Bellingham Herald ghost newspapers.

For the newspaper of a state capital to have such a small staff and feature so little coverage is especially problematic for news operations who rely on its resources for information and content.

In late December 2020, the Salish Current newspaper reported that journalists at the papers in Bellingham, Tacoma, Olympia and Tri-Cities had authorized the Pacific Northwest Newspaper Guild to represent them in forming a union. The Current article quoted a Tweet from Herald reporter Kie Relyea: "Since 2008, I've seen a lot of talented people leave as newsroom jobs were slashed. Now there are six of us trying to cover a county of nearly 230,000 people seven days a week."[39]

Chatham Asset Management newspapers in Wa

Newspaper	County	City	Daily/ Weekly	Purchased From	2004 Circulation	2022 Circulation	Increase/ Decrease
Tri-City Herald	Franklin	Kennewick	Daily	McClatchy	41,666	25,663	↓
The News Tribune	Pierce	Tacoma	Daily	McClatchy	127,928	54,000	↓
The Peninsula Gateway	Pierce	Gig Harbor	Weekly	McClatchy	9,500	4,993	↓
Puyallup Herald	Pierce	Puyallup	Weekly	McClatchy	21,900	27,000	↑
The Olympian	Thurston	Olympia	Daily	McClatchy	33,848	17,401	↓
The Bellingham Herald	Whatcom	Bellingham	Daily	McClatchy	23,938	13,073	↓

Figure 13   Purchased September 2020

"You furnish the pictures and I'll furnish the war,"
William Randolph Hearst reportedly cabled artist Frederic Remington.

Credit: "Maine war poster" by Tim Evanson (CC BY-SA 2.0)

Mis- and disinformation

The year was 1897 and Frederic Remington was in Cuba, then a colony of Spain, on assignment for the Hearst-owned New York Journal. Eager for battle between the United States and Spain, the publisher envisioned that a war would spur newspaper sales and make the young United States a more visible world player. Hearst's rival, Joseph Pulitzer, publisher of The World, held similar sentiments.[40]

It would be another year before the USS Maine exploded in the Havana harbor, eventually leading to war. But in the meantime, Hearst and Pulitzer beat the drums for battle, producing the unethical reporting known as yellow journalism.

The Journal, for example, titled its story about the Maine explosion, "The War Ship Maine was Split in Two by an Enemy's Secret Infernal Machine." The World produced equally bogus and inflammatory reporting. Later investigations concluded the tragedy, which claimed 268 lives, most likely was not the result of an attack, but an explosion inside of the ship, perhaps generated by coal dust.

Disruptive and destructive mis- and disinformation is nothing new, as this history from more than 100 years ago illustrates. Scores of other misrepresentations, from U.S. Sen. Joseph McCarthy during the early 1950s to government leaders during the Vietnam war, confirm that fake news is nothing new.

Misinformation is false or misleading information that may be spread unintentionally. In contrast, disinformation is misleading or false information that is spread intentionally, with the author aware of its false or misleading nature. This is particularly problematic on social media and online platforms because of the nearly instantaneous and worldwide reach of the internet.

"It spreads, and it spreads so quickly," observed Jaime Bodden, managing director of the Washington State Association of Local Public Health Officials, whom the study committee interviewed. We saw that during the COVID-19 pandemic, Bodden said.

"Suddenly you see somebody who has 10,000 followers on a social media site who is more of an 'expert' than somebody … who has been in the trenches of COVID and has been a public health doctor for a very long time," she said.

About half of Americans get news on social media at least sometimes

% of U.S. adults who get news from social media …

Often	Sometimes	Rarely	Never	Don't get digital news
23%	30	18	21	7

Note: This chart is not comparable to similar questions asked in the past due to question wording changes; see Appendix for more details.
Source: Survey of U.S. adults conducted Aug. 31-Sept. 7, 2020.
"News Use Across Social Media Platforms in 2020"

PEW RESEARCH CENTER

Figure 14

And for public health officials and others tasked with setting the record straight, social media "is incredibly hard to combat and reframe and reset," Bodden noted.

False narratives spread faster, farther

Massachusetts Institute of Technology research confirms Bodden's observations. According to the study, reported in a 2018 article in Scientific American, false information posted on Twitter spreads faster and farther than truth.

"False news … is on average about 70% more likely to be retweeted than information that faithfully reports actual events," according to the study. The study identified false news as inaccurate information presented as truth or opinion presented as fact. [41]

Researchers reviewed 126,000 news stories tweeted between 2006 and 2017 by 3 million people. "Accurate stories rarely reached more than 1,000 people, yet the most prominent false-news items routinely reached between 1,000 and 100,000 people," the study said. Political news spread more than three times faster than news about terrorism, natural disasters, science, urban legends or financial information.

The researchers created an algorithm that weeded out tweets by bots, concluding that people – not machines – were largely responsible for the practice. The researchers only studied Twitter, but said they suspect a similar scenario plays out on Facebook.

Nevertheless, Americans continue to rely on social media for news. (Figures 14 and 15) Half of U.S. adults surveyed in a 2020 Pew Research Center study reported they get news from social media "often or sometimes." A third of respondents said they primarily turn to Facebook, followed by Reddit and YouTube.[42]

That's even though most respondents doubt the accuracy of social media reporting. "About six-in-ten of those who at least rarely get news on social media say they expect that news to be largely inaccurate, while 39% expect it to be largely accurate," Pew reported.

The closure and reduction of local newspapers has resulted in social media and talk radio becoming primary news sources for many.

Washington State University professor Nancy Deringer encountered that problem during the COVID-19 pandemic while she was recruiting volunteers for the youth organization 4-H, for which she is a state director. "You reach out to volunteers and they tell you, 'I'm not going get vaccinated because talk radio told me it's not safe,'" she said.

WSU's Benjamin Shors said one of the problems with social media is that it doesn't do enough to ferret out mis- or disinformation.

"Many turn to Facebook or social media where there really are no repercussions for publishing false information," the professor said. Traditional news outlets take a different tack. "If you're the local newspaper and you got something wrong, you issue a correction, and that just doesn't happen in the digital spaces."

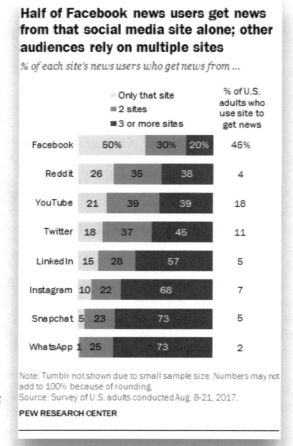

Figure 15

News consumers should learn how to judge the credibility of news sources, according to two digital media literacy instructors at Arizona State University.

"Read widely on things that interest you. Don't stay with single sources. Diversifying our information diet, or consuming information from a variety of sources, is one of the most powerful choices we can make to combat disinformation," said Dan Gillmor, one of the ASU journalism experts. "Ask your own questions. If you do that, you've made a good start."

Gillmor and his colleague, Kristy Roschke, have launched a free digital media literacy course called "Mediactive: How to participate in our digital world."[43]

Roschke said media literacy should be a life-long effort. "When we think about literacy, we think of reading and writing. I really strongly believe that you cannot be a functioning person in society if you don't understand how to interact with technology, information and, more specifically, media. I advocate for students learning about media literacy from the earliest grades all the way through adulthood."[44]

See A Deeper Dive for the value of media literacy and a list of media-literacy links

Pink slime looks like legitimate news

Yellow journalism was born in the 1800s, but it has a present-day sibling: pink slime.[45]

Pink slime publications feature the names of the communities where they appear and masquerade as both accountable and local sources of news. But they are produced by larger companies using underpaid freelancers and computer-generated content. Often they promote extreme political perspectives. Many feature copy from legitimate publications that has been altered.

As communities across the country see their newspapers close or shrink, the environment has proved to be fertile ground for pink slime, according to the Tow Center for Digital Journalism. In 2019, Tow reported 450 pink slime news sites existed.

The following year, Tow reported the number had tripled,[46] and by 2021, multiple dark money groups were providing financing as the publications partnered with advocacy groups before the 2020 election.

The owner of one of the largest companies, Metric Media, told a reporter for the Deseret News in Salt Lake City that the goal of his company "is to rebuild and democratize community news across the country."

Brian Timpone added: "We believe the disappearance of community news has contributed to a marked decline in civility in America. When Americans know about their neighbors' wedding anniversaries, their work promotions, and their children making the honor roll at school or earning junior-high basketball accolades, they are less likely to caricature and typecast each other over political issues."[47]

> There were 450 [pink slime] sites in CJR's December 2019 report, but that number had nearly tripled to 1,200 eight months later.
> — Columbia Journalism Review

Writing in the Feb. 20, 2020, Atlantic, McKay Coppins described the publications this way: "At first glance, they look like regular publications, complete with community notices and coverage of schools. But look closer and you'll find that there are often no mastheads, few if any bylines, and no addresses for local offices."[48]

Furthermore, Coppins said, the publications have pointed political agendas, which include "a scheme to exploit the credibility of local journalism."

In an interview with the news study committee, Erica Weintraub Austin, director of the Murrow Center for Media and Health Promotion Research at Washington State University, warned of the growth of pink slime publications. People who aren't media literate are being manipulated by its creators, she said.

The Metric Media network has 1,200 websites nationwide and calls itself the "largest producer of local news in the United States." However, the news sites are funded by "political actors, big-money interest groups and ideological partners that target key battleground states on certain issues, while ignoring the bigger local news stories," according to an investigation published in Columbia Journalism Review. There were 450 sites in CJR's December 2019 report, but that number had nearly tripled to 1200 eight months later.[49]

The company's website lists 22 Metric Media LLC publications in Washington state as of September 2022.[50]

The fact-checker website Media Bias/Fact Check rates Metric Media as a "questionable source," saying "Overall, we rate Metric Media LLC right-center biased and questionable based on a lack of transparency, the publication of false information, and nondisclosure of over 1,000 imposter websites that are designed to look like local news sources."[51]

See A Deeper Dive for a list of pink slime publications in Washington

Social media's positives

Despite its drawbacks, social media provides potential value to communities and local newspapers.

Shors said social media can be a positive experience for a community when news options are limited. From rural Montana, Shors is a member of a Facebook newsgroup called Blackfeet News that serves a Native American tribe. "There's great information being conveyed in that community," he said. "People become sort of community news leaders and some are fairly well trusted and accurate and they have taken it upon themselves as citizen journalists to inform."

Often in these communities, where social media creates what Shors calls a healthy media environment, the local librarian or someone associated with a school might serve as the site administrator. But absent someone to vet the postings, misinformation can spread quickly.

In Ellensburg, the Daily Record publishes four days a week and is mailed, not delivered to homes, often arriving early in the afternoon of the day it is published. But more people turn to Community Connect on Facebook for their news. The Daily Record's circulation as of late April 2022 was 5,523, while Community Connect has 12,900 reported members who live in Kittitas County.

Readers contribute content for Community Connect, to which other readers add or correct. Some contributors post personal opinions and use the venue to promote political points of view, which traditional news outlets would typically label as opinion.

Consider, too, the power social media has extended to scores of movements, starting with the Arab Spring, and continuing with Occupy Wall Street, MeToo and Black Lives Matter.

The Pew Research Center reported in October 2018 that the #MeToo hashtag was tweeted 19 million times in the year after actress Alyssa Milano urged victims to share their stories.[52]

Initial reporting identified Twitter as a key organizing tool during the Arab Spring uprisings but subsequent studies indicated the more substantial role Twitter played was communicating with audiences outside of the Middle East.[53]

Among journalists, social media can be a valuable tool to both deliver and collect news.

Journalists report that they find news sources on social media. It's a "really important platform for me in just communicating with sources and finding people to interview," one reporter said. Social media also can enable a journalist to keep closer tabs on developing news. "You find something out via Twitter or social media, whether it's looking at a player's Instagram story or someone DMs you a tip," said one Arizona sports reporter.[54]

Social media also helps promote stories. "It's driving traffic. It's driving readership," said a digital editor at The Seattle Times. "Those social media platforms have created an infrastructure ... where we can try to take that conversation and meet our readers there."

Verification is valued in newsrooms

"If your mother says she loves you, check it out" is a bit of advice that many journalists hear early in their careers. The phrase can be traced back more than 50 years to editors at the Chicago City News Bureau who insisted their reporters check and double check their facts and refrain from publishing content that hadn't been confirmed by at least two sources.[55]

News organizations and independent journalists today have varying standards for verifying information prior to publication. Some will publish what they identify as breaking news based on reports from a single source, depending on the source and what they know of the source's motive for sharing the information. Others require more vetting before they publish.

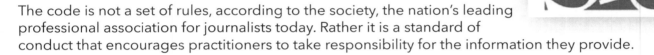

Journalists prefer to be first to report news, but most reputable reporters and news organizations – those whose work is viewed as fair and factual – are guided by a code that emphasizes accuracy and values the truth: The Society of Professional Journalists Code of Ethics.[56]

The code is not a set of rules, according to the society, the nation's leading professional association for journalists today. Rather it is a standard of conduct that encourages practitioners to take responsibility for the information they provide.

Crafted by the society in 1973 from a document prepared by the American Society of Newspaper Editors in 1926, the code has been revised four times. The updates reflect changes in society and the news industry, including those that are the result of the internet, social media and the proliferation of work by citizen journalists.

Four principles form the core of the code:

- Seek truth and report it.
- Minimize harm.
- Act independently.
- Be accountable and transparent.

In each case, the code goes on to explain each principle in more detail. SPJ officials have debated whether to take action to enforce the principles, ultimately deciding not to, based on the rights to free speech and free press guaranteed by the First Amendment to the U.S. Constitution. Instead, society leaders count on an informed public making their own decisions about what is responsible journalism, based on the principles outlined in the code.

Impact on politics

Suppose they held an election but nobody bothered to run?

That's what almost happened in rapidly growing Gig Harbor, one of several cities to lay claim to the title of gateway to the Olympic Peninsula. When the mayor decided not to seek reelection in fall 2021, the vacuum nearly went unnoticed. The News Tribune, published 15 miles away in Tacoma across the Narrows Bridge, had cut back its coverage of Gig Harbor. Political news in the South Puget Sound town was hard to come by.

"Somehow, it missed the public's eye ... that nobody was running for mayor," former state Rep. Pat Lantz, now president of the new nonprofit news website Gig Harbor Now, told the study committee in early 2022.

Less news, fewer candidates

One prominent nation-wide study of the relationship between newspaper decline and politics considers candidate participation. The 2019 study looked at local newspapers in 11 California communities over 20 years. Studying 256 mayoral races, researchers Meghan Rubado and Jay Jennings concluded cities where newspapers saw sharp staff cuts had significantly fewer candidates for mayor. The study also found that lower newspaper staffing might be a contributing factor to lower voter turnout.[57]

Rubado said the reduction in coverage and candidate participation was no coincidence. "If there's nobody reporting on or providing information about candidates, about legislation, about how money is being spent, or the budgeting process, how will people know that they require a quality challenger to unseat an ineffective mayor?" Rubado asked. "They don't know the mayor is ineffective!"[58]

The study also concluded:

- The number of candidates in an election would increase if news staff were added.
- Mayoral races were closer in communities where newspapers had more robust newsrooms.
- Communities where newspapers had larger staffs had fewer unopposed candidates.

Meghan Rubado

In England, government-backed research has identified a link between newspaper circulation and voter turnout. The study by the Department for Digital, Culture, Media and Sport concluded increases in newspaper circulation result in increases in voter turnout.[59]

To gauge the situation in Washington state, the news study committee interviewed public officials, researchers, and journalists involved in elections and politics.

In Kittitas County, Auditor Jerry Pettit said he believes fewer candidates are running for office, although the situation isn't "rampant." He doesn't blame a decline in local news. Pettit believes candidates are deterred by having "to put themselves out there." Campaigning and being public officials can make people feel as if they are living in fishbowls. The requirement to disclose financial information to the state deters some, too, Pettit said.

Travis N. Ridout, director of the School of Politics, Philosophy and Public Affairs at Washington State University, said he hasn't encountered studies beyond Rubado and Jennings' work. But he said their findings make sense to him. "I find it highly plausible that the reduction in news coverage of politics and policy at the state and local level … is leading fewer people to consider running for office," he said.

Ridout explained in an email: "Most basically, when there is less information available about the functioning of a school board, city council or state legislature, it leads to fewer people with interest in the government body's activities – and fewer people willing to run for office."

Travis Ridout

In Bellingham, Ron Judd, the editor of the Cascadia Daily News, said he believes a decline in local news is responsible for a decline in political engagement.

Judd referenced an election in November 2015. All four open seats on the Bellingham City Council featured one candidate, as did three of four races for the Bellingham School District Board of Directors. The assessor, auditor, sheriff and treasurer all were unopposed.[60]

Voter turnout decreases

Brier Dudley, who writes the Free Press column at The Seattle Times, took note of Yakima County's November 2021 election and drew a connection between voter turnout and declining newspaper staffing and coverage.

"Difficult market conditions forced the downsizing of the Yakima Herald-Republic in recent years and civic engagement is declining," Dudley wrote.[61]

"In November's election, voter turnout was an abysmal 32%, the second worst showing among Washington's 39 counties. Only Franklin County, where the Tri-City Herald slashed its newsroom even further, saw a worse turnout of just 29%. Turnout was even worse in Southeast Yakima, where just 14% of voters in District 2 participated in the City Council election. Of the district's 4,332 registered voters, only 619 voted."

Dudley also reported many people were unfamiliar with local issues. Their lack of knowledge was due to a variety of reasons, including their preference for television, which featured more national political coverage.

League committee members sought another method to gauge voter participation in Washington state, comparing turnout in three presidential election years from 2008 to 2021. We presumed voters who took time to participate in an election for a school or fire bond or levy were more committed to their communities. So we compared turnouts in the first special elections of those years, not the more popular November general elections. (Figure 16)

In all but one of Washington's 39 counties, voter turnout decreased from 2012 to 2020. In some

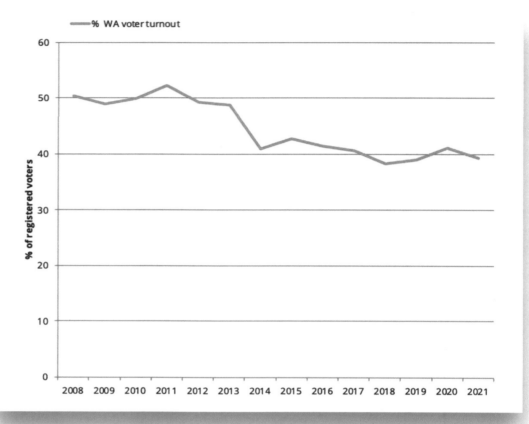

Voter participation in February county special elections 2008 to 2021

Figure 16 - News Study Committee

To consider the premise that the decline in local newspapers has had an effect on voter turnout, committee members reviewed turnout in each county from 2008-2021, focusing on the February special elections. Turnout in an election for a school or fire bond or levy might more accurately measure true civic involvement than the turnout in a heavily publicized election, such as a November general election.

In all but one of Washington's 39 counties, voter turnout decreased from 2012 to 2020. In some counties, the decrease was significant: nearly 13% in Asotin County and more than 11% in Benton County. No newspaper is published in Asotin County, although the area is served by The Lewiston Tribune. Elsewhere, the decrease was minor, such as in Skagit County, where the decrease was less than 0.3%.

counties, the decrease was significant: by nearly 13% in Asotin County and by more than 11% in Benton County, for example. No newspaper is published in Asotin County, although the area is served by The Lewiston Tribune. Elsewhere, the decrease was minor, such as in Skagit County, where the decrease was less than 0.3%.

See A Deeper Dive for data, Washington special-election voting 2008-2021

Increased partisanship

A number of studies by national scholars provide insight into the local news decline's impact on political partisanship. In an article for FiveThirtyEight, Joshua Darr of Louisiana State University wrote that he and his colleagues discovered greater partisanship was prompted by readers having available less local coverage. As a result, readers turned their attention to national sources. "In the absence of local news, people are more likely to vote for one party up and down the ballot.[62]

"When people read news about their neighborhoods, schools and municipal services, they think like locals," Darr wrote. "When they read about national political conflict, they think like partisans. In our research we found that less local news meant more polarization," he wrote.

Rowland Thompson, of the Allied Daily Newspapers of Washington, said he has witnessed greater political polarization in the state. "People are becoming more and more siloed," he said. Additionally, Thompson said he has seen a different type of candidate emerge in recent years. "In the last decade, the composition of the Legislature has changed... people used to come up through school boards and county elected officials. The real trend is now through community activism."

Josh O'Connor of Sound Publishing said divisions are becoming increasingly evident. "By taking the middle road on issues and upholding democratic values, we're finding that we're not connecting with either side because of how polarized our country has become. They don't see us as being truthful anymore."

Social media makes a poor substitute for the local newspaper, O'Connor said. "You would be shocked at how little people really understand about this process today. Many are going to Facebook for their news, and they can't distinguish the difference between a trusted journalistic voice versus something that's been shared 100 times through a post developed by a neighbor."

M. David Lee III, executive editor of the statewide news website Crosscut, said news organizations also have become more partisan over the past 10 to 15 years. "People will find a news organization that they trust, and then that's all they will focus on. They're less likely to go out and hear other points of view. And for democracy, for me, that's concerning," he said.

It's a democracy problem

Washington State University's Benjamin Shors said the changed newspaper environment has so affected politics and government that the situation isn't just a journalism problem. "It's a democracy problem. I absolutely believe that," he said.

Echoing that voters have become more partisan, Shors said a nationalization of media content means "everything becomes a referendum on Biden or Trump or on the Democrats or the Republicans." Because of the lack of local news coverage, "there's not this sort of shared community."

Shors said national coverage is conflict driven, while local news is more community driven. "It was more about here are the pictures of the local volleyball team or meet the candidates or a new pastor has moved to town and here's a vote that the local commissioners took on something. But it

Benjamin Shors

wasn't a conflict," he said.

Jacob Grumbach, a professor of political science at the University of Washington who specializes in state politics and voting, spoke of "the backsliding of democracy."

Despite the interest at the national level, much of our political future depends on what occurs at local and state levels, including election certification and decisions on voting standards and practices, he said.

The decline in local news means fewer people know who their state legislator is — or what a candidate stands for, Grumbach added. "It's all about symbolics and not real policy. It's completely obscure who stands for what."

Some researchers say newspaper dominance began to wane back in the 1950s with the advent of television. "We've long seen alarmist headlines about the death of local journalism," said Michael Sinkinson from Yale University's School of Management. Even then, citizens began showing less interest in local politics as they turned their attention to national news.[63]

Political science professors Danny Hayes of George Washington University and Jennifer Lawless of the University of Virginia wrote that the effects of the newspaper crisis are widespread.[64]

It's not just the least politically interested, but everyone has less knowledge and participates less, they reported. As newspapers falter, readers become less informed. The researchers found 70% of news readers could name their mayor in 2017, but that number was down to 55% by 2019.

Impact on civic engagement

As a teen and young adult, Lee Shaker watched with fascination the historic transformation of the media: the rise of cable news, the growing consumption of video games and the expansion of the internet.

The lightning-fast changes so mesmerized him that he wrote his 2014 college thesis on the connection between newspaper declines and civic engagement.

"Dead Newspapers and Citizens' Civic Engagement" details Shaker's study of 18 major metropolitan areas during 2008 and 2009. They included Seattle and Denver, which lost the Seattle Post-Intelligencer and the Rocky Mountain News, respectively, during that period.

Lee Shaker

Shaker, now a Portland State University communications professor, discovered civic engagement in those two cities dropped significantly from 2008 to 2009. It was a decline, he said, "that is not consistently replicated over the same time period in other major American cities that did not lose a newspaper."

Shaker used data from the Current Population Survey, sponsored by the U.S. Census Bureau and the U.S. Bureau of Labor Statistics, to track five civic engagement activities that he said help make a community healthy and successful:

- Contacting or visiting a public official to express an opinion.
- Buying or boycotting a certain product or service because of the social or political values.
- Participating in a school group, neighborhood or community association.
- Participating in a civic organization such as Lions Club.
- Participating on a committee of any group or organization.

Shaker said four of the five civic engagement indicators declined significantly in Denver, where the Rocky Mountain News closed in early 2009 after publisher E.W. Scripps was unable to locate a buyer.

In Seattle, where the 146-year-old Post-Intelligencer ceased its print publication in March 2009, two of the five indicators decreased significantly, Shaker reported.

The professor also incorporated data about whether people read newspapers, hosted household dinners, and spoke with and performed favors for neighbors.

"Newspapers are vital institutions in our democracy, and their decline warrants our concern," Shaker concluded.

Studies have linked reductions in local news coverage with greater political partisanship and less voter and candidate participation. Credit: Vesperstock (Shutterstock)

Shaker's work is the only local study specifically reporting on the link in Washington state between newspapers and civic engagement. But other studies offer additional insights.

Research in 2020 by Nick Mathews from the University of Minnesota detailed observations from 19 people after the closure of the 99-year-old Caroline Progress newspaper in Caroline County, Virginia.[65]

A ban on travel from selected countries with large Muslim populations prompted a protest in a park in Olympia, drawing media coverage. Credit: Joanne M. Lisosky

Mathews said readers missed gatherings and reported increased isolation and diminished civic pride. "Findings also show the impact on residents' daily lives, with one participant declaring 'life is harder' without the newspaper," he wrote.

A 2016 Pew Research Center study reported people who were more engaged in their communities were more interested in local news. Researchers looked at attachment to one's community, voting, activity in local and political groups, rating of the local community, and political diversity.[66]

Shaker studied the impact of the closure of a paper on a community. But he told the committee that a ghost newspaper — a paper that fails to report on significant issues and developments because its staff has been reduced so significantly — can create a situation more "insidious" than when a newspaper closes.

That's because ghost newspapers create a false sense of reality, Shaker said. Multiple studies detail the high trust readers historically have had in their local newspapers, he said. So, readers of ghost newspapers are often left assuming all is well in a community. "Until you have lead in the drinking water, you assume things will be fine," Shaker explained.

Similarly, when a community loses its newspaper or is left with a ghost newspaper, people often turn to Facebook or other social media for information. Shaker emphasized one of the problems with that: Social media audiences receive content pushed to them by algorithms created from established reading choices, resulting in a reenforcement of a reader's preconceived biases.

Additionally, compared with established local news publications, social media has a poor track record in the areas of accuracy and mis- and disinformation.

Benjamin Shors, the WSU professor, said a community loses shared values when it loses its newspaper. "There are several good studies out there … on this sense of shared community values being disrupted. Because we don't have a place where you can write a civil letter to the editor as opposed to reposting a meme that's not about your local community but about Joe Biden or Donald Trump."

Shors said some communities without a local newspaper have other venues that serve them well. Shors, who is from rural Montana, pointed to an Indian reservation Facebook group called Blackfeet News, of which he is a member.

"There's some great information being conveyed in that community. It's really a robust community that sort of self-polices. Hundreds of people within that community post content and it's a pretty healthy media ecosystem," he said. Newspapers used to provide communities with similar robust media ecosystems, he said.

In Ellensburg, more people turn to Community Connect on Facebook than the local newspaper for their news. The Daily Record, which has reduced coverage, is published four days a week now and is mailed, not delivered to homes.

The most recent circulation count for the Daily Record was 5,523, while the Community Connect site reported 12,900 members. To access the Community Connect site, one must live in Kittitas County.

Community Connect relies on reader-reported information, which is corrected by way of reader vetting. Some contributors post personal opinions and use the venue to promote political points of view, which traditional news outlets would label opinion.

Mary Snapp, vice president of strategic initiatives at Microsoft, explained why her company and other tech giants are providing support to local news operations, including the Yakima Herald-Republic. Her comments appeared in a December 2021 Herald-Republic article, "Democracy is at stake when local news sources decline."[67]

> "You don't have the local newspaper not just covering local politics, but doing something simple as saying there's a potluck in the park on Saturday or there's a community event and everyone can go."
> — Benjamin Shors

Strong local newspapers strengthen communities by bringing them together, Snapp said, "We really see a decline in essentially the local democracy of a community, but we also see a decline in the soul of a community" without local newspapers.

Lisa Bryan is executive editor of the nonprofit Key Peninsula News. The newspaper's website says the publication is "the glue that holds the community together." In an interview with the news study committee, Bryan credited the candidate forums the News helps sponsor with fostering civic engagement.

"People who attend the candidate forums and the candidates themselves say there's nothing like the turnout. It's huge, people are interested, they want to meet their candidates and they want to ask questions," she said.

Gig Harbor suffered from a lack of local coverage after the Gannett Co. shuttered its weekly Gig Harbor Life in 2018 and staff cuts at The News Tribune caused The Tribune-owned The Peninsula Gateway to reduce its coverage. After the Gig Harbor Life closed, the editor and a reporter founded the online Gig Harbor Now. The nonprofit 501(c)(3) is supported by grants and donations from readers and provides local coverage.

Pat Lantz, one of Gig Harbor Now's founders, explained the motivation for creating the paper: "If we don't have a way of informing and engaging people in their community and in their civic decision-making, who knows what's going to happen? And so, with a sense of urgency, we just went to work."

Pat Lantz

In rural Pierce County, real estate broker Emmy Lay has read the Eatonville Dispatch for 30 years. She lamented the paper's decline of coverage of community and school events.

Lay recalled the difficulty she encountered getting the local paper to cover the annual 9/11 Day of Service in Eatonville, which she chaired. Initially, the paper provided extensive coverage, but that diminished over time. "I could not get anyone from the Dispatch to return my calls and emails. I went in person to get info about the upcoming event placed in the paper, and it was like pulling teeth to get it done," she said.

Elaine Godfrey of The Atlantic magazine addressed the impact diminished coverage of such events has on a community. "These stories are the connective tissue of a community; they introduce people to their neighbors, and they encourage readers to listen to and empathize with one another," Godfrey said.

"When that tissue disintegrates, something vital rots away. We don't often stop to ponder the way that a newspaper's collapse makes people feel: less connected, more alone. As local news crumbles, so does our tether to one another."[68]

See A Deeper Dive to understand algorithms

Impact on public health

Mark Larson, Kittitas County's public health officer, recalled an article in the local newspaper from several months earlier. It was about an upcoming memorial service for a well-known elderly couple, Frank and Charlot Beard. Charlot had died in August 2020 and Frank two months later.

Frank Beard had been active in the local rodeo association and so it made sense the memorial was being planned for an indoor facility at the fairgrounds. But it was early in the COVID-19 pandemic. And Larson knew the event was likely to draw scores of the couple's friends, including many older adults.

"Many of the people who would attend were going to be in their 90s and many were likely not to be vaccinated," Larson said. The news about the upcoming event allowed the public health director to take action. He reached out to the family and fairgrounds officials and recommended changes to make the event safer.

"We worked at increasing ventilation and to put more of the service outside," Larson said. In retrospect, Larson said he wonders if perhaps he should have moved to get the family to cancel the event. Either way, he is thankful for the news article. "Without the newspaper, without me reading about it, I would not have ever known," he said.

Public health researchers and practitioners are responsible for identifying and preventing disease for the public at large. They say newspapers provide them with reliable, two-way communication they need to interact with the public.

One method the World Health Organization recommends for dealing with infectious disease outbreaks is "event-based surveillance." It involves tracking news articles about community trends and activities, as Larson did in Kittitas County.

After seeing coverage of an upcoming indoor memorial service in the (Ellensburg) Daily Record, Dr. Mark Larson contacted organizers about taking COVID precautions. Credit: Rodney Harwood, the Daily Record

Helen Branswell, a senior journalist writing for STAT, said the newspaper decline has made event-based surveillance more difficult. Her report said computational epidemiologist Maia Majumder, then a doctoral candidate at the Massachusetts Institute of Technology, sounded the first alarm. The epidemiologist said regions of the United States identified as news deserts could leave gaps in crucial data about disease outbreaks.[69]

"We rely very heavily on local news," said Majumder, now a faculty member at the Computational Health Informatics Program at Harvard Medical School and Boston Children's Hospital. "And I think what this will probably mean is that there are going to be pockets of the U.S. where we're just not going to have a particularly good signal anymore."

John Brownstein, a co-founder of HealthMap, a disease-detection project at Boston Children's Hospital, said local news reports helped in early tracking of the 2009 H1N1 flu outbreak in California. "Local media is the bedrock of internet surveillance – the kind of work that we do in terms of scouring the web looking for early signs of something taking place in a community," he explained in Branswell's article.

Branswell reports similar outcomes with event-based surveillance on outbreaks of the mumps in Arkansas in 2016-17, of SARS in China in 2003, and of changes to the global distribution of the Zika virus.

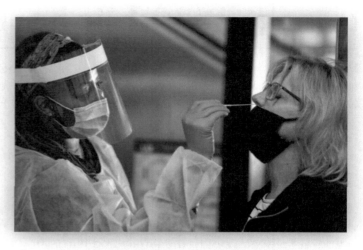

Several public health officials told the news study committee that lack of local news coverage in some regions made addressing the COVID-19 pandemic more difficult. Credit: Ringo Chiu (Shutterstock)

A correlation between loss of local news outlets and public health outcomes has yet to be quantified, but several researchers whom Branswell interviewed expressed concerns about the decline's impact.

"It is well known that event-based surveillance depends on healthy, local journalism," said Dr. Larry Madoff, former editor of ProMED, another internet-based outbreak reporting system. "So, it would be a reasonable assumption that the loss of local sources would increase the time required to discover an outbreak."

The COVID-19 outbreak, however, did prompt the Columbia Journalism Review to report on concerns of public health officials over their observations about the decline's impact on tracking infectious diseases. The October 2020 article outlined a situation where damage to robust local news reporting during the pandemic could limit detection of future disease outbreaks.[70]

"We're caught in an increasingly murky feedback loop that leaves us more aware of the system's limitations – but less prepared to address them," author Lauren Harris wrote.

Meanwhile, in an April 2020 Brookings Institute report, research analyst Clara Hendrickson wrote that the pandemic negatively impacted news operations across the country, illustrating a sobering impact of the news decline. "While the COVID-19 pandemic underscores the critical need for local journalism, it threatens its provision," Hendrickson wrote.[71]

Many rural communities and historically underserved populations such as Native Americans long have suffered from news deficits, and the pandemic hit those audiences especially hard. Further, the development was made worse by declines in hospital beds and medical services. "It is impossible to know what will not be told in the communities that have seen local newspapers disappear in recent years, but undoubtedly, important stories will go uncovered as the coronavirus spreads across the country," Hendrickson wrote.

Pulitzer Prize- and Emmy award-winning journalist Hedrick Smith, who reported for The New York Times for 26 years, spoke at a fundraiser for the Salish Current in Bellingham in March 2022. He said COVID-19 illustrated the need for solid local news coverage.[72]

"I can't think of a time in American history or certainly during my own half century as a journalist when the need for local news was more acute," Smith said. Details about where to get shots and medical advice had to be dealt with on a community basis, he said.

In Washington state, Kittitas County's Larson and Bob Lutz, the former public health officer for Spokane County, discussed in separate interviews the role local news plays in public health. Lutz is presently public health officer for Asotin County.

Lutz summed it up this way: "One of the things that public health officials do during an emergency is provide correct information and confidence to their community that things – I won't say are under control – but that there are people and organizations that are monitoring and trying to keep them safe."

Both officials repeatedly spoke of community, trust, and communication as underpinnings of successful public health programs. Solid newspapers foster all three, they said.

Bob Lutz

Lutz discussed how public health in Spokane County responded proactively to a significant hepatitis A outbreak a few years ago. "Through journalism, we found out where some of the problem spots existed," Lutz said.

And local reporting in Spokane was valuable during the pandemic as well. "I would learn about a business that was flaunting masks or occupancy," Lutz said. "I learned about a bar in Spokane Valley that, in spite of limited occupancy, was wide open. I'm sure there were other examples. And how I learned about it was by reading about it in the newspaper."

Despite the value of newspapers, both officers said they have witnessed a decline in people turning to local publications. Larson spoke specifically to times following President Donald Trump's election. "The number of people who are interacting with us through the newspaper has really gone down since the 2016 election," he said.

Mark Larson

Both blamed the shift for a loss of trust and open-mindedness as well as increased anger and the promotion of preconceived ideas. Larson specifically identified social media for much of the last development. Too often, social media creates feedback loops in which people "are just listening to the things that reinforce what they already believe." During the pandemic, Larson said, social media generated resistance to public health measures, including masking and vaccinations.

Both health officers said they work actively to nurture relationships with reporters to try to offset that impact. In Spokane, Lutz said the community benefits from the work of a Spokesman-Review journalist who reports exclusively on health and public health issues.

As a result, Lutz said, readers began to see more clearly what a public health program can provide a community. "Prior to the pandemic, people would say public health is there to serve the indigent. And they think of public health as regulatory such as with restaurant and school inspections. That we tell people what they can't do."

The relationship enabled the public health department to raise awareness about other important issues, Lutz said. "I discussed climate change and race equity, and when Spokane sponsored an HIV conference, I had a chance to talk about HIV. It gave me a chance to introduce people to the idea that public health is more than regulation and taking care of the underserved." Lutz and Larson said newspapers provide greater balance, objectivity and reliability than other venues where people get their news.

News stories also can humanize situations. Lutz said The Spokesman-Review's coverage of immigrants from the Marshall Islands and their customs and practices helped reduce prejudice and fostered greater community.

Lutz said newspapers can help build community another way. "The local newspaper, at least in our county, is pretty good at looking at both sides of the discussion. And then the back and forth that happens between people who respond to articles is really helpful," he said.

Larson said the exchange made possible in a reputable newspaper allows readers to know the people they are debating, resulting in more civil discussions, as opposed to anonymous social media posts that can be more inflammatory. "It's harder to be angry with someone when you're looking them in the face and you realize that they're really a neighbor and they really do care," he said. "If we lose our local paper, we lose a tool for public health, an unbiased tool for public health in a small community."

Jaime Bodden, the managing director for the Washington State Association for Local Public Health Officers, said social media has filled in as an information source in the wake of the closures and reductions of many local newspapers. Bodden said social media can be good or horrible. "And right now, because of COVID, it seems particularly horrible," she told the study committee.

"In terms of the misinformation that's there, it spreads and it spreads quickly," Bodden said.

At Washington State University, Erica Weintraub Austin directs the Edward R. Murrow Center for Media and Health Promotion Research. She described the changing local media landscape as presenting both opportunities and challenges.

Jaime Bodden

"There is so much information, but also so much disinformation," Austin said. "You have to be media literate and even for people who are media literate, it is challenging. Information is changing, science is changing and unfortunately you don't have consistent messages from government experts."

Austin noted the decline of print newspapers requires people to turn to the internet for information, but rural areas of Washington don't always have reliable access. "If you don't have a good internet connection and many people in rural Washington don't, you are often listening to angry talk radio and getting a lot of misinformation," she said. Austin said some of the misinformation is innocently shared. "Maybe it's just now out of date. But some disinformation is purposefully shared and often for political reasons."

Impact on public finance

The tiny, densely populated California city of Maywood caught the interest of Los Angeles Times reporter Ruben Vives after he learned about impending layoffs of almost all city employees. Financially beleaguered Maywood planned to outsource city services to Bell, an adjacent city of similar size and demographics.[73]

Soon after, Vives' partner on the story, Jeff Gottlieb, discovered that the county district attorney's office had opened an inquiry into unusually high salaries being paid to Bell City Council members. The lead investigator told the reporters that the part-time city council members, who he said should be earning a $400 monthly stipend, instead were being paid more than $8,000 per month, or nearly $100,000 per year.[74]

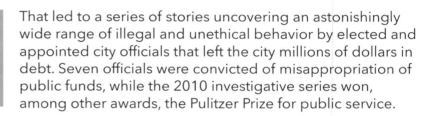

City council members, typically paid $400 per month, instead were being paid more than $8,000 per month.

That led to a series of stories uncovering an astonishingly wide range of illegal and unethical behavior by elected and appointed city officials that left the city millions of dollars in debt. Seven officials were convicted of misappropriation of public funds, while the 2010 investigative series won, among other awards, the Pulitzer Prize for public service.

Although a blogger had accused Bell city officials of corruption for years, and residents had badgered city hall for answers about excessive taxes, nothing slowed the malfeasance until the story made the front page of the Times.[75]

"I do think there's a connection between having less local journalistic oversight over local government, and whether or not there is effective government at the local level," Mike Pellicciotti, Washington state treasurer, told the news study committee. "One of the most important roles of government is the distribution of public funds. Without good journalism and good oversight, you lose that public watchdog component."

Indeed, when newspapers close, it costs more to run local government, according to a 2019 Hutchins Center on Fiscal and Monetary Policy study of the impact of newspaper closures on public finance. Government costs include more employees and higher wages, increased county deficits per capita and higher tax revenues per capita.[76]

Higher government costs lead to higher borrowing costs for cities and counties, the study said. A typical municipal bond to pay for construction of a hospital or school can cost as much as 11 points more in the wake of a newspaper closure. This means taxpayers will pay an additional $650,000 in interest payments over the life of a bond, based on an average bond size and duration of $65 million over 10 years.

Mike Pelicciotti

Dermot Murphy, one of the three authors of the Hutchins Center report, told the news study committee, "When we were starting this paper, our idea was that if there's no longer a watchdog in the community, it's possible that government might be more prone to raising taxes or increasing deficits, or simply just hiring more employees than necessary."

The study concluded that "local newspapers hold their governments accountable, keeping municipal borrowing costs low and ultimately saving local taxpayers money."

Michael Craw, master of public administration director at The Evergreen College, said, "One could argue that local newspapers play a role in holding local officials accountable for the fiscal performance of local government, and so when local media coverage is more robust, local officials have more reason to behave in ways that are fiscally responsible." The director continued: "This in turn might give bond rating agencies more confidence that local bonds will be repaid and reduce borrowing costs."

Murphy said certain conditions make fraud more likely to be discovered. "We don't see an effect when you go from four [newspapers] to three, because there's still plenty of good investigative reporting being done, and there is robust competition," he said. "If you're in a one-newspaper town, there might be less motivation to be competitive about getting the story first and in the highest quality manner."

Dermot Murphy

In Murphy's study, the authors observed that newspapers sometimes have a financial incentive to avoid investigating corporate misconduct, especially when corporations lend significant support to the newspaper's owners via ads or other means. This deterrent does not exist in government coverage.

However, a 2021 Journal of Financial Economics study concluded that scrutiny by local newspapers also has an impact on corporate behavior, finding that the closure of local newspapers caused corporate misconduct to increase. [77] "Local facilities increase(d) violations by 1.2% and penalties by 15.2%. Taken together, our findings indicate that local newspapers are an important monitor of firms' misconduct," the study authors concluded. The misconduct covered in the report includes violations of workplace safety, environment, labor relations, employment discrimination, securities and consumer protections.

Washington Attorney General Bob Ferguson believes corruption — whether public or private — thrives in darkness. "A healthy investigative press makes it more likely that the public hears about this corruption," Ferguson wrote in an email to the committee.

Ferguson said the decline in local news coverage has made his work more difficult in several ways. "My office receives more than 24,000 consumer complaints per year. These complaints often lead to positive resolutions for consumers, who receive an average of $4-6 million per year from our informal complaint resolution process," he said.

Bob Ferguson

Investigations based on these complaints can also lead to lawsuits that produce nationwide corporate reforms and millions of dollars in restitution for consumers, Ferguson said. He relies on traditional media to publicize the office's services, but he worries that residents who can no longer pick up a local newspaper won't know where to complain about deceptive business practices.

One of Ferguson's highest profile cases came out of a news clipping he read about Motel 6 in Arizona routinely sharing guest information with federal immigration enforcement. He wondered if the same thing was happening in Washington state.

After an investigation showed that was the case, Ferguson filed a consumer protection and civil rights lawsuit in January 2018. Motel 6 paid out a $12 million settlement and adopted nationwide reforms. About $10 million went to the affected Washington families. Without local news reports, fewer residents will know to file for restitution, Ferguson said.

"Thomas Jefferson may have said it best when he wrote that 'a properly functioning democracy depends on an informed electorate.' I agree," Ferguson said. "Local news is the vehicle through which we stay informed. It is essential to the health of our states, communities, and our democracy."

In October 2021, Ferguson led a bipartisan coalition of 15 attorneys general asking Congress to pass the Local Journalism Sustainability Act. "We must do all we can to save local journalism," he said.

See A Deeper Dive: Malheur Enterprise digs into finance

Television's accountability reporting

Newspapers generate the bulk of original accountability journalism, but television news provides some impressive coverage. One needs only to check out recipients of the National Academy of Television Arts & Sciences' Emmy Awards in the Pacific Northwest. On display is quality investigative work by KING, KOMO, KPTV, and KIRO, to name a few.

Local television news is financially stronger than newspapers. One reason is that every two years a tidal wave of political campaign money provides strong revenue streams. The average local TV station has more news employees than the average American newspaper, and local TV news remains the dominant news source for Americans, according to a Knight Foundation study.[78]

Local TV news is positioned at the top because its competition, namely newspapers, faces such monumental changes. Meanwhile, radio, the report noted, is neither growing nor shrinking. However, Knight researchers also portray how local TV news falls short. They advise specific improvements: "Drop the obsession with crime, carnage, and mayhem. And focus on ways to connect with local communities through a focus on issues such as education, the economy and transportation."

Knight researchers urge the coverage that experts, including Federal Communications Commission officials, identify as critical to building strong communities, and for which quality newspapers have been known: reporting on health and welfare, emergencies, jobs and business, education, transportation, civics and politics.

Benjamin Shors, the Washington State University communications professor, said TV news has historically focused on breaking news, but some broadcast and digital-native outlets, including nonprofits, are doing solid work. He pointed to efforts by local TV news to expand their websites, particularly those that are employing journalists trained in accountability journalism. Some are among the recipients of 2022 Northwest Emmy Awards from the National Academy of Television Arts & Sciences.

Podcasts are a growing source of solid journalism, including work by two Pacific Northwest journalists, Leah Sottile (Bundyville) and Ashley Ahearn (Women's Work, Boise State Public Radio). KING television news in Seattle has twice won the Kenneth F. Bunting Award, in 2017 and 2020, for outstanding journalism from the Washington Coalition for Open Government. The coalition recognized the station and reporters Susannah Frame and Chris Ingalls "for exceptional journalistic work that supports and demonstrates the importance of open government."

The Responses

Community partnerships

Seattle Times Co. president Alan Fisco didn't hide his exuberance as he described a fundraising campaign at the Yakima Herald-Republic, which the Times owns.

"Our vision for this partnership has not been tried anywhere else," Fisco wrote in a Dec. 7, 2021, article in the Herald-Republic.[79] "If successful, Yakima's coverage will thrive, serving the Yakima community like never before."

Fisco and others involved in the two-year-old Yakima Free Press Community Journalism Fund campaign are seeking to raise $1 million over the next five years from Yakima residents and large donors.

Fisco's colleague, Times publisher Frank Blethen, said the goal is to more fully serve the community by hiring more journalists at the Herald-Republic and El Sol de Yakima, its Spanish-language sister paper.

Whether the outcome will be successful is unclear. At this point the effort is noteworthy — and not only for the sizable target. The drive exemplifies a dramatic shift for news outlets, which until the 2000s were able to rely on advertising sales and subscriptions to balance their budgets. Other community fundraising campaigns are underway at newspapers serving Seattle, Everett, Spokane, Tacoma, Vancouver and elsewhere. A number, but not all, have resulted in impressive participation and contributions.

Frank Blethen

The Yakima push began in 2020 after the Microsoft Corporation granted funds to the Yakima Valley Community Foundation for training, business software and other technology at both newspapers and Radio KDNA. The financial boost enabled the outlets to produce significant reporting on missing and murdered Indigenous people, health care access and COVID-19, foundation president Sharon Miracle wrote in the Herald-Republic. [80]

The foundation hosted public gatherings where leaders emphasized that losing the paper would lead to dire consequences for the community. Meanwhile, volunteer advisers began planning ways to sustain journalism in Yakima.

Miracle explained the goal: "A sustainable model for local journalism to thrive and serve our community – not just newspaper subscribers, but all residents, with free access to critical local news." In a January 2022 column, Herald-Republic editor Greg Halling outlined the plans.[81]

Editors intend to hire a team of four reporters to focus on health care, public safety, social and economic issues and agriculture. Two of the four will be Report for America reporters, meaning their salaries will come from RFA and local donors. After that, two other reporters, whose salaries will come from the campaign, will cover education and local government.

"Then, as soon as funding allows, we'll put together a second essential news desk – this time, a team of bilingual reporters whose mission is covering the Valley's Hispanic community," Halling wrote.

He said essential work produced by reporters financed by the campaign will be available for free to all readers online, explaining, "Essential news is of little value if it isn't easily and widely accessible."

Under publisher Blethen's direction, the Times has been involved in community-funded journalism for about a decade, creating the Education Lab in 2013, then adding the Traffic Lab for transportation issues, Project Homeless, the A.I. Age (artificial intelligence), and most recently, the Investigative Journalism Fund, raising a total of $5.5 million from corporate donors and philanthropic foundations.[82]

The Herald-Republic project is an extension of that community-funded journalism, an attempt to extend community funding to rural areas, according to Brier Dudley, the Times Free Press editor.

"It was the next iteration, taking the models we developed here in Seattle and extending them to rural areas," Dudley said. The Seattle model has been so successful that other newspapers in Washington are adopting the ideas and catching up to the Times, he said. Community fundraising for the Times' newsroom pays for 27 positions in a 120-person newsroom, Blethen said.

In Tacoma in 2019, The News Tribune's Pedersen also announced the launch of a fundraising effort to expand education coverage in Pierce County.[83]

"The News Tribune will allocate resources to provide news coverage and/or investigative reporting, above and beyond routine coverage and operations, intended to inform, explain, and educate the public regarding educating our children in a coronavirus world," she wrote.

Pedersen encouraged readers to make a tax-deductible gift to support The News Tribune by sending a check to the Local Media Foundation, a nonprofit organization that works to sustain more than 3,000 news outlets nationwide.

For whatever reason, however, Tacoma has not experienced the same results as the Times in Seattle and elsewhere. A News Tribune website indicates a campaign for donations to a Coronavirus Reporting Fund closed two years ago after 394 supporters contributed $42,125 to a $82,000 goal.[84] Another News Tribune campaign to raise $20,000 to provide in-depth coverage of how local schools adapted to the pandemic ended a year ago, with 88 supporters giving $6,435.[85]

About 130 miles south, in Vancouver, The Columbian was preparing to launch a similar push when the committee interviewed Innovation editor Will Campbell in early February 2022. Campbell's great-grandfather, Herbert Campbell, purchased the paper in 1920, making Will and his brother, Ben, the publisher, fourth-generation owners.

Like The News Tribune, The Columbian partnered with the Local Media Foundation to collect tax-deductible donations to hire additional reporters.

The foundation allows for donations of all sizes, from large sums from established organizations and philanthropists to small gifts. "So, anyone who wants to donate as little as $5 can contribute to local journalism," Campbell said.
.

At The Spokesman-Review, Rob Curley said community support is foremost. But also particularly important is letting donors know what their support pays for – and that it's not to "help old rich white guys get richer."

Brenda Mann Harrison

Besides fundraising campaigns, the effort to enlist community support includes hosting events like the Northwest Passages reading forums, which bring a variety of speakers to Spokane. Curley solicits contributions from the community at these events. He also noted that a request to support local journalism appears at the bottom of stories in The Spokesman-Review. An online reader can contribute with a few clicks.

Meanwhile, The Daily Herald in Everett, part of the Sound Publishing Co. chain, has created a new position to help nurture community financing. Brenda Mann Harrison is the paper's journalism development director.

She said key to obtaining donations is letting people know that the newspaper crisis "is a crisis for our democracy and that communities suffer without coverage of important issues that affect them."

A goal of the Herald's partnership with the Community Foundation of Snohomish County is to raise $250,000 to pay for investigative reporting. The long-term goal is to raise $550,000 to establish a trust to retain at least one full-time reporter, according to Report for America.[86]

At least three newspapers in Washington have partnerships to help young people develop a better understanding of journalism. At The Seattle Times, Dudley, the Free Press column editor, is involved in programming to educate high school and college students about the role of the press.

In Spokane, Curley created a paid internship program for high school students who work alongside professionals in the newsroom. And in Vancouver, The Columbian offers a paid summer internship to a qualifying student from Clark College.

See A Deeper Dive for Will philanthropy save the day?

Nonprofits

As previously mentioned, it was the recognition that local coverage creates a sense of community that motivated a former Gig Harbor Life editor and reporter to secure support from community leaders to launch the nonprofit online Gig Harbor Now in September 2021.

"We were going to lose our history and our community, our civic engagement that have been fostered for all these years, through a reliable local newspaper," said Pat Lantz, the former legislator who is now president of Gig Harbor Now.

"There was nobody covering City Hall, there was nobody covering the council meetings, until we started doing it," added treasurer Jenny Wellman. Lantz said the community had no way of knowing how the COVID pandemic was affecting local schools, either.

"There was no way that anyone but an engaged parent would learn anything about what the protocols were for getting your kids to and from school, taught virtually or not," she said. "And right now, we've got a whole lot of depressed kids, but there was no way that the school district could engage the public for assistance or the public could express their empathy and offer assistance."

Jenny Wellman

Gig Harbor Now provides a full lineup of local coverage: community, arts and entertainment, business, education, environment, government, breaking news, sports and transportation.

The Rotary Club and the Greater Tacoma Community Foundation provided about $20,000 in grants and individuals donated additional funds. "We had a really immediate response from the community," Wellman said. "The hunger is real" for factual information, Lantz added. "I think we have been surprised at how easy our mission has been telling people about it, because you connect with this hunger."

Gig Harbor Now is one of eight nonprofits to bring a new business model to Washington journalism, allowing publications to supplement – or replace – advertising revenue with grants, donations, and memberships.

Lantz said the nonprofit model "gives us a kind of cachet as being, from the get-go, truthful, fact-based and honorable in the profession. … What kind of conflicts could there be? Someone can't buy you because that's not the way you're operating."

Representatives from five Washington nonprofits the committee interviewed in early 2022 said they were making ends meet, though fundraising remained a continual challenge. Some rely on volunteer reporters and editors, while others pay key employees and hire freelancers. Full-time newsroom wages range from $36,000 to $60,000 annually, and per-story pay for freelance reporters varies from $100 to $5,000, depending on the story and the publication.

Other Washington news nonprofits range from hyperlocal Key Peninsula News, The JOLT and the Salish Current to InvestigateWest, which serves the "Pacific Northwest and Cascadia," and Crosscut, with a staff that spans the state. (Figure 17)

Nonprofit news outlets in Washington

Publication	Format	Frequency	Focus
Crosscut	Online	Daily	Statewide politics, culture, equity, environment
Gig Harbor Now	Online	As stories are ready	Pierce County local news
Grist	Online	Several days per week	National environment, social justice, poverty, hunger
InvestigateWest	Online	Once or twice per week	Investigative reporting for the "Pacific Northwest and Cascadia"; environment, health and wellness, social justice.
Key Peninsula News	Online/Print	Monthly	Pierce County local news
Salish Current	Online	Several days per week	Local news in San Juan, Skagit and Whatcom counties
The JOLT	Online	Daily	Olympia, Lacey and Tumwater local news
Yes!Media	Online	Daily	National social justice, environment, health and wellness.
	Print Magazine	Quarterly	

Figure 17 Credit: News study committee

See A Deeper Dive for What is a nonprofit and more state nonprofit outlets.

The Institute for Nonprofit News

The nonprofits all are members of the Institute for Nonprofit News, a national organization that provides coaching, tools and services such as its popular NewsMatch financing program. Through NewsMatch, the INN matches money that news organizations raise locally. In 2021, INN's partners provided nearly $4.8 million in matching funds to 275 news organizations.

Before becoming an INN member, news organizations must meet strict standards of independence, ethics and financial transparency. The INN has more than 400 members and itself is supported by grants and donations from foundations and individuals, according to its website. [87]

Sue Cross

The first U.S. nonprofit news publication was Mother Jones, the investigative journalism magazine that launched in 1976, said Sue Cross, the INN's executive director and CEO. By 2009, there were about 30 publications and websites, including Seattle's InvestigateWest, she said.

In September 2022, nonprofit news received a shot in the arm with a donation of $4.75 million to the INN Network from the John S. and James L. Knight Foundation.

In a news release, the institute reported that the funds will be used to increase the number of nonprofit newsrooms from 400 to 600 over the next four years and boost revenue from more than $400 million to $1 billion annually.

The INN said the funds would be directed to help member news operations "expand their audiences, advance leaders of color, and attract new business and editorial talent to the growing field."[88]

Big Tech contributions

Sen. Maria Cantwell didn't hold back in October 2020 as she addressed the chief executive officers of Facebook, Google and Twitter at a U.S. Senate committee hearing.

"Today, I expect to ask the witnesses about the fact that I believe they create a choke point for local news," the senator said at the Commerce Committee hearing. Not long after, the committee, which Cantwell chairs, released a report identifying "unfair and abusive practices by major tech platforms that have contributed to the drastic revenue declines" of newspapers.[89]

"The biggest online platforms unfairly use content, take local news consumer data, and divert customers away from local news websites, while providing little in return," Cantwell declared.

Not surprisingly, the Big Tech companies responded.

Google refuted the descriptions of its role in the decline while it acknowledged the business model faces "enormous challenges."[90] The tech giant pointed to its plan to pay $1 billion to publishers around the world for their content.

And Facebook replied by stating that "local news is critical to an informed society" and noting the company had committed $400 million to local news efforts, including $100 million to help news organizations affected by COVID-19.

Many people who blame Big Tech for contributing to the decline of local news say such financial support is designed to deflect complaints, generate good public relations and stave off legislation that could hurt them financially.

> "If it hadn't been for Microsoft money, we would have been forced to reduce the size of our reporting staff."
>
> — Greg Halling

Several media analysts and news business executives told Reuters that funding from Big Technology firms "does not nearly compensate for the tens of billions of dollars publishers lost as the tech companies gobbled up the digital advertising market."[91]

But the article also reported some of the sizable contributions the companies have made to local news efforts across the country and around the world.

As of mid-2021, for instance, Facebook and Google each had directed $300 million to programs to support local news efforts. Other news reports detailed additional giving. Plus, the companies said they would continue to support local news efforts once current financing expired.

The Reuters article also reported Big Tech had dedicated $1 billion to news outlets to pay for content the news organizations produce, but which the tech companies post. The article noted that Reuters itself had received $19 million in grants from Google and $4 million from Facebook in 2020.

Microsoft is behind two efforts in Yakima. The first involved helping kick off the $1 million community fundraiser to expand local news coverage at the Herald-Republic and its Spanish-language sister paper, El Sol de Yakima.[92]

The goal of the Yakima Free Press campaign, under the umbrella of the Yakima Valley Community Foundation, is to hire 12 journalists to provide essential news coverage, all of which will be accessible for free online.

The second Microsoft contribution is its Journalism Initiative, which editor Greg Halling said involves a financial component as well as training for Herald-Republic and El Sol staff members on a range of Microsoft software products. The training has led to significant reporting improvements, including the ability to craft graphics, charts and maps that add important context.

"The training has made our reporting more effective, richer, more accessible and engaging," he said. "We're able to share information at a glance that would be difficult to provide in text."

Halling was candid about Microsoft's support.

"Microsoft is a tech company and understands it has played a role in the landscape that has developed in the last few years," he said. "It understands it needs to take corrective measures. It has a social conscience and understands that journalism is vital to a democracy and to making sure there is news to deliver."

Greg Halling

Halling said Microsoft's contributions had already made a measurable difference and had allowed the paper to retain newsroom staff and produce its deeply reported coverage on missing and murdered Indigenous people.

"'If it hadn't been for Microsoft money, we would have been forced to reduce the size of our reporting staff and we don't have any room to give – it would have been devastating," he said.

Microsoft is behind similar efforts in Fresno, California; Jackson, Mississippi; El Paso, Texas-Ciudad Juarez, Mexico, and Appleton, Wisconsin. The tech giant also is partnering with Report for America to support five newsrooms in Kansas, Oklahoma, Arizona, California and West Virginia.

Mary Snapp, vice president of strategic initiatives at Microsoft, explained the company's reasons for the support in the Yakima Herald-Republic. The demise of a local newspapers, she said, leads to "a decline in essentially the local democracy of a community … (and) a decline in the soul of a community."[93]

In a question-and-answer report in the paper, Snapp elaborated: "We actually think of newspapers as critical in our society and our ability as a company in a democratic society to do the job we need to do for our customers. If we don't have a healthy journalism sector in our society, people won't know what's real and what's not real."[94]

The Seattle Medium, which serves the African-American community in that city, has been a Google beneficiary. In 2021, The Medium was one of more than two dozen papers selected to participate in a six-month Google News Initiative Ad Transformation Lab."[95]

The lab is a collaboration with the Association of Alternative Newsmedia, the National Association of Hispanic Publications and the National Newspaper Publishers Association. It provided coaching and instruction to help publishers maximize digital advertising and content distribution, The Medium's publisher Chris Bennett said. "So, if you were to do a Google search and typed in 'African-American Seattle,' it would make it so articles we posted would populate more readily."

The lab also prompted The Medium to switch to a Google advertising platform, a system that Bennett described as particularly efficient and robust. He said he can't put a dollar figure on the assistance Google provided, but it has been meaningful. "Traffic to our site is up," he said.

In early 2022, The Skanner, which serves Black communities in Seattle and Portland, learned it was among 15 participants in a second Google ad lab.[96]

Google's support also comes in the form of backing for other initiatives, like Northwestern University's Medill Subscriber Engagement Index, to which the tech giant awarded $500,000.[97]

The index is an analytics system that allows newsrooms to track online reader engagement. At The Columbian, subscription marketing manager Sierra Myers said using programs such as the engagement index is an industrywide practice. "We are becoming more customer driven," Myers said.

In 2018, meanwhile, Facebook launched a $3 million pilot to help local newspapers improve their digital subscription models. The Seattle Times was among the participants in the Facebook Journalism Project: Local News Subscriptions Accelerator.[98]

The following year, Facebook announced plans to contribute $300 million to local news operations for more assistance with subscription models, reporting grants for local newsrooms and investments in nonprofit local news operations. Funds also were targeted for news literacy programs and fact-checking efforts.[99]

Then in 2020, Facebook, by then identifying as the Meta Journalism Project, contributed another $100 million to support local newspapers, including $10.3 million to 144 newsrooms in the United States affected by COVID-19.

Among the Washington state recipients of Facebook support that year were Cascade Public Media/ Crosscut, which received $46,000; InvestigateWest, $32,545; Nguoi Viet Tay Bac/Northwest Vietnamese News, $73,000; The Seattle Times, $150,000; the Wahkiakum County Eagle, $35,000; and the Yakima Herald-Republic, $100,000.

In 2019 Facebook agreed to three-year deals with The New York Times, The Washington Post and Dow Jones, parent company of the Journal, to publish content. Facebook has paid average annual fees of $15 million to the Post, more than $20 million to the Times and more than $10 million to the Journal.

But in late July 2022, Axios reported Facebook was telling its partners that it planned to halt its practice of paying leading news organizations to permit Facebook to publish their content on its news tab. According to Axios, funding to 50 publishers wasn't going to be renewed.[100]

Legislation

In many ways, U.S. Rep. Dan Newhouse and Sen. Cantwell couldn't see things more differently.

Representing Washington's 4th Congressional District, a Republican stronghold that includes Yakima and the Tri-Cities, Newhouse is known for his conservative credentials. He has earned an "A" rating from the National Rifle Association, opposed ending hostilities against Iran and has pushed to halt federal financing for Planned Parenthood.

Cantwell represents a state that hasn't elected a Republican governor since 1981 and for the last 28 years has sent only Democrats to the U.S. Senate. She has an "F" rating from the National Rifle Association, sought to end hostilities against Iran, and supports funds for Planned Parenthood.

But the two have found common ground on the Local Journalism Sustainability Act. Both are original sponsors of the bill, which would offer tax credits to local readers, advertisers and news producers.

Maria Cantwell

"At its core, local news is about holding the powerful accountable," Cantwell said in 2021, when she, Mark Kelly, D-Arizona, and Ron Wyden, D-Oregon, introduced the bill in the Senate. "The strength of our democracy is based in truth and transparency, and local newsrooms are on the ground in our communities asking the critical questions, countering misinformation, and telling our stories."[101]

Newhouse sounded a similar refrain when he and Rep. Ann Kirkpatrick, D-Arizona, introduced their version of the bill in the House. "Local journalists and newspapers are essential to ensuring the public remains informed," he said.

Newhouse also addressed how the measure might benefit remote areas, like those he represents. "Local news is crucial – particularly within our rural communities in central Washington – and our local journalists provide in-depth perspectives that inform their readership regarding local current events," he said.[102]

Dan Newhouse

The act is one of a handful of federal bills crafted in response to the local newspaper crisis. Others, including the Future of Local News Act and Saving the Local News Act, promote government support for news outlets and consequently have generated debate about the appropriateness of that provision.

The federal Journalism Competition and Preservation Act differs from the others in that it does not call for government support. It would protect news outlets from antitrust legislation and allow them to band together to negotiate with Big Tech companies on distribution terms of the news companies' content. It is often referred to as the Safe Harbor act.

Seattle Times publisher Frank Blethen credits Washington legislators at the federal level for their support of local news. "The Washington state delegation is so heads above in terms of knowledge and commitment to a free press than any other delegation, and that goes back to 20 years ago when we were enlisting our senators to help us repeal a death tax exemption for family newspapers."

No federal legislation has won approval, but there's been success at the state level. Describing those efforts as gaining momentum, Tim Franklin, director of the Medill Local News Initiative at Northwestern University, pointed to legislation that has resulted in the creation of a task force in Illinois to study the crisis, a tax-credit measure for advertisers in Wisconsin, and funding in New Jersey for innovative media and civic-technology projects that support coverage in news deserts.[103]

Government support issues

Some who oppose government support argue newspapers should stand on their own: If newspapers can't survive the turmoil of the free market, perhaps they should change their business practices.

In January 2022, state Sen. Lynda Wilson, R-Battle Ground, expressed that sentiment during a Business, Financial Services & Trade Committee hearing on a proposal to eliminate the business and occupation tax for newspapers: "I know newspapers are on the downside. But if we did this for every business that was failing, like manufacturing …" she said.[104]

Many companies and corporations benefit from government support to a great degree. In 2015, for instance, Washington aerospace manufacturers received preferential tax rate reductions totaling $90.5 million, and aerospace non-manufacturers received tax credits totaling $99.8 million.[105]

The majority of local newspaper owners and publishers surveyed by the news study committee expressed support for the Local Journalism Sustainability Act.

But not all in the news industry agree. In New York, Jeff Jarvis, director of the Tow-Knight Center for Entrepreneurial Journalism at City University, said, "I see danger everywhere if government funds or in any way approves or interferes with journalism and speech. To accept funding from government, no matter the alleged safeguards, puts us at risk of mortal conflict of interest."[106]

Closer to home, in Pomeroy, Charlotte Baker and her husband, Loyal, produce the East Washingtonian and the Dayton Chronicle. Baker said she could not accept government support because doing so would compromise the integrity of their journalism.

See A Deeper Dive for a story about the East Washingtonian
See A Deeper Dive for a table of proposed legislation, descriptions of those acts, and a sampling of legislation in other states

Other government support

The advent of broadcast news led to the 1967 Public Broadcasting Act, which set aside parts of the broadcast spectrum for public radio and television and created a U.S. Treasury fund to pay for the operation of the channels.[107]

Many people mistakenly think the federal government fully finances public broadcasting. But it pays for only about 15% of U.S. public broadcasting funds, and that percentage changes yearly.[108]
The 1992 passage of the Cable Television Consumer Protection and Competition Act requires cable television systems to devote channels to local commercial and public broadcast stations.[109]

Additionally, the Federal Communications Commission, created in 1934, regulates radio, television, wire, satellite, and cable, and has taken action affecting newspapers. In 1975, the FCC passed the newspaper and broadcast cross-ownership rule prohibiting common ownership of a full-power broadcast station and a daily newspaper in the same market. The rule was overturned in 2017.[110]

Historical government support

Those who favor financial government support point to examples of how newspapers for years have benefitted from such financing. And they also note that the press is the only private institution that is protected in the U.S. Constitution.

"Congress shall make no law respecting an establishment of religion, or prohibiting the free exercise thereof; or abridging the freedom of speech, or of the press; or the right of the people peaceably to assemble, and to petition the Government for a redress of grievances," the First Amendment reads.

Seattle Times publisher Frank Blethen believes the First Amendment was created "to protect the people's press from the people's new government."

In the statement of purpose for the Free Press Initiative, Blethen said, "Our Founding Fathers recognized that in all cultures and societies, it was the wealthy and powerful who understood the value of news and information. Consequently, they sought control and selectively withheld information from the population."[111]

Blethen added, "Our Founders also recognized the average citizen could not afford, nor was willing to pay for, news and information. In their brilliance, they understood it would take government protection and subsidization to ensure the creation of a robust press free from government interference and control by the rich and powerful."

Federal, state and local governments have supported news publishers with tax breaks, postal subsidies and the printing of public notices as far back as the country's founding – and even earlier. Benjamin Franklin, as postmaster, ensured a low postal delivery rate for newspapers throughout the 13 colonies. After that came Congress' long-running support for low-cost – sometimes free – delivery of periodicals. Congress legislated postage rates until 1970, subsidizing "postage on periodicals by over-charging for letter postage and, when necessary, digging deep into the U.S. Treasury."[112]

In 1970, The Postal Regulatory Commission began oversight of the Postal Service, gradually reducing postal subsidies by more than 80%. And today, another long-time source of revenue for newspapers is in danger. Government agencies want courts to allow them to switch to the internet to publish public and legal notices.[113]

The federal government stepped in with large scale investment to help create the internet, and continues to provide funding for broadband improvement, unintentionally helping divert consumers from print and broadcast outlets to the web.

Government should explore ways to support the production of news and information as it has done throughout history, according to the authors of a 2010 University of Southern California paper on public policy and funding the news.

"We do not favor government policies that keep dying media alive," the authors said, but asked, "Is a new form of government intervention prudent, and necessary, to ensure that Americans have access to the kind of information they need in a democracy? If there is such a need, is government capable, amid such overwhelming change in the news business, of making choices that will make things better?"
The report suggested government provide support of news production with the following caveats:

- Most government funding should be indirect, rather than direct.
- Funding should be distributed according to a formula rather than directly to news outlets.
- Reporters, news organizations and content creators should be paid for work that would otherwise be used without compensation.
- The government can provide support by investing in technology and innovation.

McChesney on government support

Robert McChesney, a well-known author who has published widely on the history, current state and future of journalism, told the news study committee that America's founders kept newspaper distribution costs low to encourage their publication. "They would then enhance the quality of our culture and it is really one of the great success stories of American history," he said.

"If you read Thomas Jefferson, James Madison, Alexander Hamilton, John Adams or Thomas Paine," McChesney said, "you will see how central having a free press system was to their vision of self-government."

In an interview on the Analysis.news site in December 2020, McChesney said support from the government "made it possible to have this plethora of diverse views in newspapers which were foundational to our political democracy, the best parts of our democracy."[114]

> "Our press system is the result of government policies. It has been from the beginning...."
> — Robert McChesney

He added, "There wasn't a single social movement of value from abolition to the suffragettes to labor ... that wasn't led by editors, that wasn't led by news media. The media was the center of democracy."

But, he noted, "By the time the commercial media giants came along in the 20th century, it was assumed that the market would always produce a huge news media."

McChesney bemoans the typical political response of "The cost is too high" when discussing government support of local journalism. He said the founders of the United States understood that journalism is a public good.

"The correct response, the one that guided our Founders, is what will the cost be if America *doesn't* do it? There are signs all around us of what that looks like," McChesney said. "The nation can no more lowball having a credible press system as democracy crumbles than it would lowball military spending in the midst of a foreign invasion."[115]

See A Deeper Dive for McChesney offers new plan for news

Finding a sustainable future

None of us has a crystal ball. But looking to the future, a number of newspaper leaders say the first order of business is to double down on local. As they hope to reverse or simply stem the tide, publishers and editors in Washington told the study committee they are committed to providing more information that readers need day in and day out - about what's happening in their cities, on sports fields, and in local theaters, stores and cafes.

Let the national papers focus more on national and international news, they say.

At The Spokesman-Review, Rob Curley started his local focus commitment with the front page.

He said a review of many local papers from across the country on a given day will turn up the same four stories, all focusing on national or international developments, and often reporting on "the worst of the worst, like here are the crappiest things that happened."

> If I can get people to come to our paper to read about [Gonzaga sports], I can get them to stay to read about what's happening at our city council."
>
> — Rob Curley

Curley said a better front page would feature "a mixture of really serious stuff … but also stories about heroes." Crooks and murderers aren't the only people who should appear on A1, he said, adding the front page should provide readers "a daily report of your community."

As he lets the national papers focus on broader news, Curley has capitalized on a topic dear to the hearts of many in Spokane – Gonzaga University athletics, specifically men's basketball. "I knew it wasn't going to be big J journalism at all," Curley said of his plans. "But I was going to go in all guns. I knew people were passionate about basketball."

Curley met with Gonzaga leaders and explained he hoped to draw people to The Spokesman-Review with extensive Bulldog coverage, and that the coverage wouldn't appear only on the sports pages. University officials welcomed the proposal.

"If I can get people to come to our paper to read about them, I can get them to stay to read about what's happening at our city council," he said. Curley likened Gonzaga sports coverage to a gateway drug that he's using "to try to help save democracy."

As they pursue the focus on all things local, Curley is not shy about asking readers for money. At the bottom of every locally produced story is a plea for support. The pitch, featuring a line that reads "local journalism is essential," notes donations help offset the cost of several reporter and editor positions.

The Spokesman-Review's commitment to local also includes a reading forum that brings speakers to Spokane. Presenters at Northwest Passages over the years have included romance writers, college professors, religious leaders, gardening experts and athletes, including former Gonzaga basketball stars.

Curley said the forums succeed even when speakers present perspectives that differ from the sentiments of most Spokane residents.

He recalled the evening an environmentalist was scheduled to speak. Before the curtain went up, Curley told the guest that nearly half of the audience was made up of ranchers. The speaker then asked Curley: "We're gonna die, aren't we?"

To the contrary, "it was an amazing evening with tons of questions and great discussion and when the light turned on, almost no one left," Curley said.

Spokesman-Review executive editor Rob Curley isn't shy about soliciting contributions for the paper: "I make no bones that that's what I'm doing." Credit: The Spokesman-Review

Later, a member of the audience asked Curley why he had created the forums. "I said I needed to bring the community together to talk about things. They need to see what journalism is about and see this author they've never seen before," he said. Curley's not shy about using the forums to solicit donations either. "The first 20 minutes is me explaining newspapers in a way that they're all laughing. I make no bones that that's what I am doing."

Curley makes it clear that contributions to support local journalism don't come with any privileges. No donors, even the more generous, influence coverage, he said. Editors make decisions on stories, including whether to publish, based on traditional news values.

Because the money to add positions comes directly from the public, the stories those reporters produce are not behind the paywall. They are available to anyone who visits The Spokesman-Review website without charge. "The work of any journalist who is funded even in part by this fund can no longer carry a Spokesman-Review copyright. It has to carry a Creative Commons copyright and everyone can own it," Curley said.

Finally, Curley said the local push also means producing stories that people who live in Spokane want and should read. He said that doesn't mean he serves readers simple-minded pieces on insignificant topics.

His standard is, "How many people other than your mom will read it?" That is, the story should be solid enough – and well told enough – that "everyone who is 12 should care about it," Curley said.

In April 2022, The Spokesman-Review sent staff writer Eli Francovich to eastern Europe to follow the work of a Spokane doctor who was helping victims of the war between Ukraine and Russia. The paper wrote: "Francovich's trip is supported by the Innova Community Journalism Fund, which holds the donations of supporters who attend the Northwest Passages events in Spokane. If you can support the newspaper's coverage of the Ukraine war, please go to spokesman.com/thanks."

As they pursue community partnerships and public fundraising efforts, experts also say it's important to tell potential donors where their money is going. That's why, in Vancouver, Will Campbell, The Columbian's innovation editor, said editors widely publicized the news that contributions from the community would be used to hire four reporters to cover homelessness, transportation and the environment.

As of late April 2022, The Columbian reported it had $1 million in pledges with a goal of raising another $650,000. Campbell said soliciting local support has become an industry standard.

Reducing print, boosting online

Improving local news coverage is a goal across the board, but a number of local news outlets are looking to cut back the frequency of their print editions to save money and to meet the preference of growing numbers of readers.

One of the earliest papers to reduce the number of days it publishes in print is also one of the country's oldest papers, the New Orleans Times-Picayune, which announced its plans in 2012 to cut back to print publications on Wednesdays, Fridays and Sundays. The then-175-year-old paper also announced that a new company, the NOLA Media Group, would oversee production of The Times-Picayune and its affiliated website, NOLA.com.[116]

In Florida, the Tampa Bay Times announced in March 2020 that the daily would publish new editions online every day but publish in print only on Wednesdays and Sundays, the most popular days for readers and advertisers.[117]

Chief executive officer Paul Tash said the paper had spent the previous two years ramping up its digital capacity "so that we can serve the audience however they come to us." He called the move a "good time to gently guide our readers toward the electronic formats." The delivery format would change, but Tash promised "the journalism is as strong as ever."

In early 2020, The Columbian stopped printing a Monday paper, though the edition is available online. The announcement cited a continuing trend in the news industry.[118] Publisher Ben Campbell noted two other Washington papers were cutting back on print, The News Tribune and The Olympian, both eliminating print on Saturdays.

As for the future at The Columbian?

Will Campbell

Innovation editor Will Campbell told the study committee that leadership had no immediate plans for further print reductions. But, he said, "eventually we will likely have to cut print."

Meanwhile, "our goal is to keep print around as long as possible because we know how important that is to our most diehard readers," he said.

But younger readers, like himself, often get their news from The Columbian's website. "I don't read the print publication every single day. It's mostly online for me," he said. Eventually he envisions a print edition one day a week with "the best stories that are more thought out and vetted that people can sit down and really pay attention to."

Columbian leadership also aims to increase digital subscriptions to a number equal to 10% of Vancouver's population, as Times leadership has done in Seattle, when they recently surpassed 80,000 digital subscriptions. "We'll be able to support the entire operation, just through digital subscriptions," Campbell said.

The Kitsap Sun, owned by Gannett, the nation's largest newspaper chain, announced in mid-January 2022 that it would eliminate its Saturday print edition. The paper is published in Bremerton and serves Kitsap, Jefferson and Mason counties. Editor David Nelson wrote, "Our present and our future is focused on reaching readers through different platforms, including a website, mobile app, e-edition and social media, in addition to the traditional paper."[119]

Moving from print to digital makes sense, said Washington State University's Benjamin Shors.

"Print has an incredibly clumsy distribution system. You get the words, you type them down, you transfer them over to a press that cost tens of millions of dollars, you print them, have somebody load them in the back of a pickup and you drive them around," he said.

At The Seattle Times, Blethen said fewer print editions with more frequently updated and robust websites are likely to be the future. When that transition will happen is not certain. "Anyone who says they know exactly what the market is going to look like is just guessing," Blethen said. He anticipates Seattle, being a large market, will continue to produce print editions longer than communities with smaller circulations.

Blethen said some papers cut print to save on distribution and printing expenses but don't match that with a boost in digital coverage. "And then they're going to try to get you to pay for a digital product which, in terms of content, is really substandard," he said.

Six years ago, the Times began studying reader demographics to ensure the news outlet was producing content to reach all ages. "We didn't want to have content driven to one group and lose the rest of the market," Blethen said. Capturing the millennial reader has been a particular goal.

In Yakima, The Herald-Republic has cut back to print three days a week. At the same time, all content produced from the newspaper's five-year fundraising campaign will be free, not behind the newspaper's paywall. Blethen noted the Yakima effort includes a push to reach the Latino community, which 2020 census numbers show is more than half of the population in Yakima County.[120]

"We need to figure out how we're going to engage more fully the Hispanic community," he said. Many stories will be translated into Spanish and appear in the Herald-Republic's sister Spanish-language publication, El Sol de Yakima.

Meanwhile, to read stories behind their paywalls, decision-makers at The Seattle Times and The Spokesman-Review both are looking at raising digital rates while increasing subscribers. "It's been fascinating to us how many people are becoming accepting of the fact that you need to pay for journalism," Blethen said.

Previously, digital growth was limited primarily to the largest papers — The Wall Street Journal, The New York Times and The Washington Post — but that's changing.

A mid-February 2022 New York Times article reported "publicly released corporate data and interviews with executives of local newspapers appear to buttress … optimism." The Times identified digital growth at regional newspapers in St. Louis, Houston and San Francisco. The Seattle Times recently exceeded 81,000 digital subscribers.[121]

Josh O'Connor

Mark Jacobs of the Medill Local News Initiative wrote in 2021 that digital success is tougher for smaller news outlets. Among the reasons Jacobs cited is limited tech support, the difficulty of tracking reader behavior, and spotty internet in rural regions. Jacobs' article also reports the observations of Nancy Lane, the chief executive officer of the Local Media Association, which supports fundraising efforts for more than 3,000 news outlets across the country.[122]

Lane said many weekly newspapers have strong support, but "they do need to figure out the digital strategy because we live in a digital world." A year earlier, in another article, Jacobs also quoted Lane. She said one of the more promising paths forward for local news outlets is a "digital subscription plus" approach, meaning philanthropy and subscriptions.[123]

Josh O'Connor, president of Sound Publishing, said the company's business model is predicated on three primary revenue lines. "One is local retail revenue. That's our ability to do business with merchants on Main Street and give them really good advertising and marketing solutions that they can use both in print and digitally. The other is growing subscription and connecting with readers so that they invest in a free and transparent media voice in their town," O'Connor said.

"The third would be growing both digital advertising revenue and digital subscription. Sound will finally crest about a million in digital subscription revenue, which I think is a really important watermark for us. We can continue to invest in more journalism jobs within these markets that we serve."

What else might the future bring?

Cross, of the Institute for Nonprofit News, said she believes the continued growth of the nonprofit news industry shows that "sustainable business models exist for journalism rooted in civic purpose rather than profit." She predicted that within 10 years, "independent, nonprofit newsrooms will produce a significant share of the news consumed by most Americans about our civic life."

Conclusion

This study makes clear the reality and consequences of the local newspaper decline in Washington state. It also makes clear the expansiveness of the decline — from major metropolitan dailies to small rural weeklies to specialized publications that serve communities of color.

The loss of staffing, the closure of newspapers and the dramatic reduction of coverage affect the communities and lives of Washingtonians. The impact is apparent in at least five areas: less civic engagement, greater political partisanship, reduced political participation by candidates and voters, higher cost of government, and negative developments related to public health.

When our founders established our country, they recognized that a free press is essential to the functioning of a democracy. Testament to that is the protection they provided the press in the First Amendment to the Constitution. The founders established it was appropriate to encourage journalism's survival in the marketplace and created mechanisms for its viability such as reduced postal rates.

As revealed by the individuals the committee interviewed and reports the committee studied, the decline of local news threatens our democracy in very real ways. That reality should prompt action by the League of Women Voters, the leading nonpartisan organization dedicated to empowering voters and defending democracy.

A League policy on news media

Although The League of Women Voters does not currently have a policy on news media, many League policies implicitly require a strong, trustworthy and reliable system — such as the local news media — to disseminate information.

Take this concept of government adopted by the national convention of the League of Women Voters:

> *The League of Women Voters believes that democratic government depends upon the informed and active participation of its citizens and requires that governmental bodies protect the citizen's right to know by giving adequate notice of proposed actions, holding open meetings and making public records accessible.*

In the national League's positions and policy guide, "Impact on Issues," the words "news" and "media" are mentioned 22 times.

National news coverage of government officials and policies, for now, remains robust. But this study points to ways local newspapers are failing in this area. Researchers have documented that the number of residents who know little to nothing about local government is soaring in communities where newspapers are shrinking and disappearing.

Certainly, local Leagues in communities across the nation continue to provide civic and voting information to the public. But like other nonprofits that educate the public about issues as diverse as the environment, culture, education, health and mental health, the League is dependent upon the local news media.

Opportunities

Some people don't appreciate that providing quality local news coverage is a costly venture. They'd rather turn to social media or access information on sites where they don't have to pay.

But as has been illustrated in Seattle, Spokane and elsewhere, people value news that informs them and helps them guide their lives. If they are encouraged to do so, people who want meaningful coverage of their communities are willing to invest in their local newspapers. Readers of publications such as The Seattle Times, The Spokesman-Review, The Seattle Medium and The Black Lens in Spokane have shown themselves to be fiercely loyal and supportive.

It's also true that some publishers continue to demonstrate their primary goal is to make money, not to contribute to an informed community. Those newspaper owners don't know, or don't care, how valuable real journalism is to a community and to democracy.

But many editors and reporters do recognize the significance of the service they provide and they are working diligently despite obstacles. Some news organizations are finding success as nonprofits, which also deserve recognition. Recognition, too, should go to tech giants like Microsoft, Facebook and Google, which have directed millions of dollars to local news operations. But the profits of those companies shouldn't be at the expense of local newspapers.

Government's role

An increasing number of federal and state elected officials recognize that government has a role in supporting a vibrant press. Washington's Sen. Maria Cantwell and Rep. Dan Newhouse are among those who have introduced important federal legislation. Congressional progress on these bills appears at a standstill, but the lawmakers' push for action is a start. A number of states are making headway, although Washington's failure to extend a business and operations tax preference for newspapers is troubling.

In December 2021, Washington's Joint Legislative Audit and Review Committee noted the expiring tax reduction for printing and publishing newspapers was not sufficient to stem newspaper losses. The committee urged the Legislature to consider additional support if it "is interested in helping the newspaper industry more broadly."

Also calling for support was the Citizen Commission for Performance Measurement of Tax Preference. Among its statements was this observation: "Local papers still support democratic and community vitality with the dissemination of local news absent from newer, national digital providers."

The citizens commission addressed another important reality: News deserts disproportionately affect rural and poor communities. While some efforts are being made to improve broadband in rural communities, those efforts are far from enough, and those communities also lack the devices with which to access the internet. So the commission's call to extend assistance to newspapers touched on a key point: "Additionally, local papers offer an alternative for residents with barriers to accessing newer digital formats."

But alas, no action was taken. The proposal to extend the tax preference failed to advance out of committee. One lawmaker questioned whether it is appropriate to support a private enterprise, apparently not considering the millions of dollars the government awards to the aerospace industry and others.

Nor apparently did that lawmaker consider the ways local newspapers contribute to a community beyond the benefits from other products that can be sold.

What else might the Washington Legislature consider in terms of assistance? Lawmakers could study other tax-relief provisions, other methods of government and non-government support and measures being taken in other states, most notably in New Jersey and Colorado, could be studied.

The main takeaway from this study is that newspapers are a public good. They are not just another business or industry. And the problem they are experiencing is not just a journalism problem. It's a democracy problem.

Quick Takes

Quick Takes recaps the main points in each chapter.

The Crisis

Numbers don't lie

- Newspaper newsroom jobs have declined 50% nationwide. Washington state newspapers lost 67% of their newsroom employees from 2005 to 2020.
- Twenty-five percent of newspapers across the country have closed since 2004. During that time, Washington lost 20% of its newspapers – more than two dozen of 140 publications.
- King County launched three newspapers but lost 11 from 2004 to 2022; Snohomish County launched two newspapers but lost nine.
- Daily and weekly newspapers nationally and in Washington have significantly reduced their reporting, including their coverage of government bodies and agencies.
- Observers describe the Olympian, the News Tribune in Tacoma, and the Herald in Bellingham as "ghost newspapers," publications where coverage is severely diminished.
- The executive editor of the Spokane Spokesman-Review described six outlying counties as news deserts when he applied for and received grant funding for a reporter to cover the region's more rural areas.
- About a dozen of Washington's 39 counties, mainly in rural areas, are served by one weekly newspaper.
- Twenty years ago, 16 full- and part-time reporters covered the state capitol. Today, five full-time reporters cover the capitol.

Causes

- People cancel their subscriptions because they think newspapers are too expensive, too boring, and too political. They also say they don't have time to read them.
- Newspapers have been slow to respond to readers' preferences for online news.
- Many papers initially were reluctant to add an online presence because they feared their operations would suffer financially.
- Prior to 2000, advertising provided 80% of a newspaper's revenue while circulation accounted for 20%. Today, it's the reverse, with advertising contributing 35% of revenue, while circulation is 65%. These changes are insufficient to cover costs.
- Online advertising generates fewer dollars than print advertising.
- Newspapers have lost significant advertising to Big Tech companies, including Google, Microsoft, and Facebook. Big Tech companies make billions of dollars from posting advertising next to news content produced by newspapers. Sen. Maria Cantwell and others label this practice as unfair and abusive.
- Big Tech companies are often blamed for the decimation of newspaper advertising and the loss of 60% of newspaper revenue since 2015.
- Nationwide and in Washington, consolidation of retailers – drug stores, markets, car dealers ,and others – has contributed to the ad revenue decline for newspapers.
- Readers often drop their subscriptions when local newspapers focus on national news over local coverage.
- Changes in ownership, often from sales of family-owned operations to hedge funds and large national newspaper chains, have resulted in significant staffing declines and major local coverage reductions.

- Chatham Asset Management purchased six Washington newspapers, three of which are now described as "ghost newspapers." Five of the six have experienced dramatic reductions in circulation.

Mis- and disinformation

- The internet allows false news to "go viral" at speeds not possible in the past. Lies spread faster and farther than truth.
- When people rely on social media for news, public health officials have encountered problems in communicating health information.
- Most people surveyed believe social media news is largely inaccurate, but they still turn to it for news.
- Traditional media outlets issue corrections for inaccurate reporting but that rarely happens in social media.
- A new phenomenon called "pink slime" allows some newspapers to look legitimate although they publish false information. They often are funded by political interests. At least 23 pink-slime publications have been identified in Washington state.
- Social media can provide a positive experience for communities, when community leaders dispense accurate news posts. More people subscribe to a Facebook group for Kittitas County residents than subscribe to the Ellensburg Daily Record.

Ethnic newspapers

- A number of newspapers for specific ethnic communities in Washington state often serve as a community focal point. Some papers, like The Medium, which serves the Black community in Seattle, host community events.
- Several ethnic newspapers in Washington have strong reader loyalty with communities that want to be engaged and involved. Despite the pandemic and newspaper challenges, 2020 was the South Seattle Emerald's most profitable year.
- Spanish-language newspapers in Washington provide important information to a growing population. El Sol de Yakima serves Yakima County, where Hispanics are 51% of the population.
- Coverage of Native American issues is limited in Washington's mainstream press, although the Yakima Herald-Republic's reporting of the murder and disappearance of Indigenous women has been strong and impactful. Additionally, three Washington newspapers share the services of a Report for America journalist who covers Native American issues.
- COVID has had an impact on staffing and advertising for ethnic papers.

The Impacts

Impact on politics

- One national study reported mayoral races were closer in communities where newspapers had more robust newsrooms; communities with larger staffs had fewer candidates running unopposed.
- No one initially filed to run for mayor in Gig Harbor, which lost local news coverage until a nonprofit came on the scene. No one challenged the incumbents in several races a few years ago in Bellingham, which also experienced reduced local news coverage.
- Travis N. Ridout, director of the School of Politics, Philosophy, and Public Affairs at Washington State University, said he believes it is highly plausible that a reduction in local news coverage leads to fewer candidates.
- Consistent coverage of local government is labor-intensive and is often the first eliminated when news staffs are cut. That impacts the public's knowledge of government issues.
- One national study reported 70% of news readers could name their mayor in 2017, but that number dropped to 55% two years later.
- National research reports voters become more partisan when local news outlets close and focus on national controversies instead of local happenings.
- Voter participation declined in every February Special County Election but one throughout Washington's 39 counties from 2008 to 2021, according to original research by the news study committee.
- WSU's Benjamin Shors said the decline of local newspapers isn't just a journalism problem. "It's a democracy problem."

Impact on civic engagement

- A Portland State University researcher studied civic engagement in 18 major metropolitan areas and reported that civic engagement dropped significantly in cities after they lost newspapers. He found civic engagement declined in Seattle after the Post-Intelligencer ceased its print publication in 2019.
- Civic engagement includes contacting a public office to express an opinion, supporting or boycotting a product or service because of political values, participating in school groups, community associations, or civic organizations, and serving on a committee of any group or organization.
- A 2016 national survey reported people who were more engaged in their communities were more interested in local news.
- When people turn to social media for news, they often don't realize they are frequently guided by algorithms to stories designed to increase "clicks," where disinformation often lives. The algorithms push them to read stories matching their preconceived biases.

Impact on public health

- Newspapers can help keep watch over health trends in the community by identifying and preventing disease.
- Several public health officials said community trust and communication are underpinnings of successful public health campaigns and newspapers help foster all three.
- Rural and under-served communities are the hardest hit in the area of public health when newspapers decline.
- The rise of the internet and more polarized beliefs have led to a loss of trust and open-mindedness on health issues, according to public health officials.
- Washington observers said nonexperts with large social media followings are often more trusted than medical experts.

Impact on public finance

- National studies report losing a newspaper can force taxpayers to pay more for higher employee wages, increased taxes, and higher county deficits. Higher government costs lead to higher borrowing costs for cities and counties.
- Washington state treasurer Mike Pellicciotti said good journalism and good oversight are important as watchdogs of public funds.
- Loss of newspapers also increases corporate corruption. Attorney General Bob Ferguson has called for legislation to support local news outlets.
- Ferguson also turns to newspapers for help in locating possible corruption, to distribute information to the public about corrupt activity, and to notify citizens they may be due restitution.
- Even when government fraud is suspected by local residents, it often takes newspaper coverage before the corrupt behavior is stopped.

The Responses

Community partnerships

- From eastern Washington to the western, northern, and southern ends of the state, newspapers are increasingly turning to both community residents and large donors to help fund additional coverage.
- Spokane's Spokesman-Review has garnered considerable community support from public events.
- Social media companies are lending a hand with grants and training to help newspapers learn about digital analytics.
- Donors like to know what their support pays for. So news outlets provide the public with details about their plans for donations.
- A handful of fiscal sponsors allow local newspapers to solicit tax-deductible donations.

Nonprofits

- Some local publications are recreating themselves as nonprofit organizations and qualify for grants that would not otherwise be accessible.
- Like for-profit publications, nonprofits face financial and funding challenges.
- The Institute for Nonprofit News is a national organization that provides coaching, tools, and services for new nonprofit newspapers.
- Washington has at least six nonprofits that provide local news coverage; others focus on investigative reporting and specialized topics. Their primary format is online.

Big Tech

- Washington's U.S. Sen. Maria Cantwell and others blame Big Tech for contributing to the decline of local news.
- Facebook, Google, and Microsoft have organized efforts to help support local news with grants, training, and fundraising. Many papers throughout Washington state, large and small, mainstream and specialized, have benefitted from this assistance.
- In Yakima, the editor of the Herald-Republic said help from Big Tech has enabled the paper to provide high-quality and impactful journalism about the death and disappearance of Indigenous women.
- Representatives of Big Tech say they understand that newspapers play a crucial part in today's world.

Legislation

- Washington Sen. Maria Cantwell and Rep. Dan Newhouse say local newsrooms are crucial components of democracy. They have proposed federal legislation to help support newspapers financially.
- Several federal bills have been proposed to support local news but none has been approved.
- Washington lawmakers declined in early 2022 to extend a business and occupation tax credit to newspaper publishers. The tax preference is set to expire in 2024.
- Elsewhere state efforts to support local news have been more successful.
- Some opponents to government backing ask why newspapers should be supported over other types of businesses. Other opponents say they see danger of government interference with journalism and speech if newspapers accept government funds.
- Proponents of government backing say the founders supported newspaper delivery from the birth of the U.S. through the U.S. Postal Service.
- Proponents also point to the number of corporations subsidized by tax dollars, including in Washington state, where Boeing receives substantial government support.
- Historians say newspapers are foundational to our political democracy.

The Future

Finding a sustainable future

- Editors of local newspapers in Washington and across the county say no one can focus on community news like local outlets.
- Across the state, readers are demonstrating support for newspapers in community fundraising efforts.
- Newspapers are reducing the number of print editions per week and boosting their online presence.
- Printing newspapers is expensive, as is the delivery system.
- The future is uncertain in Washington state and across the country.

In ac libero augue, lacinia   ullam ut nisl at metus pel-   Aenean nec ipsum risus.   In ac libero augue. Aliquam erat volutpat.
elementum lorem. Donec   lentesque molestie. Ut ut   Vivamus posuere mi in   lacinia elementum lo Phasellus hen drerit.
elit felis, pharetra ae gravida   ante lectus. Mauris cursus   libero aliquet sit amet con-   rem. Donec elit felis, libero   et   consequat

A Deeper Dive

Lorem ipsum dolor sit   ullam ut nisl at metus pel-   scurabitur elit iellus, elcifend   Proin nisi mi, varius   Vivamus libero lectus,
amet, consectetur adipse-   lentesque molestie. Ut ut   ut   ultrices   scelerisque,   nec blandit eget, mollis a   luctus vitae dapibus id.

The plight of The News Tribune

The decline of The News Tribune in Tacoma, once one of the fastest growing newspapers in Washington, provides a timely example of the state of local news today.

The paper was established in 1883. The Baker family purchased it in 1912 and produced a civic-minded newspaper for nearly 75 years. The News Tribune printed a number of regional and national papers at its in-house plant.

In 1986, McClatchy Newspapers purchased The News Tribune (along with papers in Bellingham, Olympia, and Tri-Cities), reportedly for more than $205 million. At the time, McClatchy owned other newspapers in California, Nevada, Washington, and Alaska.

David Zeeck began work at The News Tribune in 1994 as a news editor. He eventually became president and publisher of McClatchy newspapers throughout the state. "When we first came to Tacoma, it seemed that every house had a News Tribune box out front. It was just everywhere," he said.

During those boom years, The News Tribune purchased new printing presses, anticipating its circulation would continue to grow. It built a huge news press bay and moved the operation to a 248,000-square-foot plant in 1997. "The prevailing thoughts of printed newspapers was that they would just keep growing. It seemed like the future was immeasurable and inevitable," Zeeck said. At its height, there were as many as 130 newsroom staffers.

Zeeck remembered Google and Facebook starting to cut into newspapers' audiences by the mid-2000s. In response, the newspaper began to "cover the heck out of local news, including almost all the school boards and any sizable city council meetings," he said. Daily circulation rose to 110,000.

Then the print hit the fan. By 2008, the recession was in full swing and owner McClatchy was in financial trouble. Many said the company had overpaid for acquiring Knight Ridder and its 32 daily newspapers in 2006.

"Everyone assumed if you could just make the transition over to digital that things would be OK," said Penelope Abernathy of Northwestern University. "But the problem was that as of 2015, Google and Facebook made up about 75% of the digital ad dollars in U.S. markets. That's not enough to sustain the newsrooms McClatchy inherited from Knight Ridder."

The News Tribune stopped printing the paper on its own press in 2018, and laid off 67 associated employees. In 2020, McClatchy filed for bankruptcy protection, citing a pension crisis and the news industry's financial challenges.

Home to the newspaper since 1974, The News Tribune building in Tacoma stands for sale after the paper was acquired by Chatham Asset Management in 2020. The 248,000-square-foot building on 13 acres sold for $15.5 million in late summer 2021. Credit: Joanne M. Lisosky

In stepped Chatham Asset Management, McClatchy's largest creditor, which acquired the newspaper company for $312 million and pledged to preserve newsroom jobs. However, staff cuts followed. At The News Tribune, the reporting has staff dropped to about 25, said Stephanie Pedersen, the current editor and president.

In 2020, Pedersen tried to raise $20,000 to increase coverage of education in Pierce County, but collected only $6,435 from 88 supporters. However, the paper has hired a reporter from Report for America to report on Indigenous communities. That reporter is shared with The Olympian and the Bellingham Herald.

In 2021, The News Tribune's building was sold for $15.5 million, with much of the staff working remotely during the pandemic.

As of March 2022, the newspaper reported average circulation of 28,454 Sundays and 27,234 weekdays, with 1.6 million monthly unique viewers online. Since 2010, the population of Tacoma has increased 12.3% to about 223,000.[124]

The News Tribune still lands on doorsteps every day except Saturday. Its website says the paper is hiring.

Back to A Table of Contents
Back to the study

Rate your local news

How effective is your local news outlet at covering your community? Whether it is a newspaper, TV station, radio, or online only, you can see how much local news your outlet contains. Learn how to use this simple rating sheet, and download your own copy:

https://www.usnewsdeserts.com/reports/news-deserts-and-ghost-newspapers-will-local-news-survive/rate-your-local-news/

HOW GOOD IS YOUR NEWS?

Rate the information you are receiving from your local news organization. The aim is to determine both the quality and quantity of the information. Over a four-day period, enter the number of stories for each day in the category that applies. The higher the total score for each category, the higher the ality of the stories in that category. Some categories may have no stories. What news are you missing?

Name of News Organization								
Categories	Emergencies and Public Safety	Health	Education	Transportation Systems	Environment and Planning	Economic Development	Civic Information	Political Life
Examples	Dangerous Weather, Accidents, Crime	Quality of local hospitals, spread of disease, availability of tests/ treatments	Quality of local schools, public funding, decision-making processes	Road conditions, mass transit, future needs	Quality of air/ water, alerts to current/ potential hazards	Major issues at local/state level, local employment	Social services, religious and nonprofit groups, libraries	Voting/ candidates, major issues, public meetings
Day 1								
Number of Local Stories About This Topic								
Number of Stories By a Local Journalist								
Number of Stories With Useful Information								
Number of Stories with Valuable Context/ Analysis								
Total								
Day 2								
Number of Local Stories About This Topic								
Number of Stories By a Local Journalist								
Number of Stories With Useful Information								
Number of Stories with Valuable Context/ Analysis								
Total								
Day 3								
Number of Local Stories About This Topic								
Number of Stories By a Local Journalist								
Number of Stories With Useful Information								
Number of Stories with Valuable Context/ Analysis								
Total								
Day 4								
Number of Local Stories About This Topic								
Number of Stories By a Local Journalist								
Number of Stories With Useful Information								
Number of Stories with Valuable Context/ Analysis								
Total								
Grand Total								

Figure 18 Credit: UNC Hussman School of Journalism and Media

Back to Table of Contents
Back to study

Washington Newspapers 2004 vs. 2022

Washington Newspapers in 2004 and 2022

The information below is current as of early 2022, and is from a variety of sources, some of which provided conflicting data. The information provides a good overview of the changes seen in Washington, however. Titles in red indicate a closure. **Bolded** names represent a new publication since 2004.

		2004				2022					
City	County	Newspaper	Daily/ Weekly	Owner	Circulation	Newspaper	Daily/ Weekly	Owner	Circulation	Increase/ Decrease	Notes
Othello	Adams	The Othello Outlook	Weekly	Basin Publishing Inc	2,000	The Othello Outlook		Basin Publishing Inc.			Closed 2021
Ritzville	Adams	The Ritzville Adams County Journal	Weekly	McFadden Stephen	1,942	The Ritzville Adams County Journal	Weekly	Free Press Publishing	2,146	↑	
Prosser	Benton	Prosser Record-Bulletin	Weekly	Fournier Newspapers	1,447	Prosser Record-Bulletin	Weekly	Vallley Publishing Co.	2,809	↑	
Wenatchee	Chelan	The Wenatchee World	Daily	World Publishing Co. (WA)	24,685	The Wenatchee World	Daily	Wick Communications (World Publishing)	15,001	↓	
Cashmere	Chelan	Cashmere Valley Record	Weekly	Prairie Media Inc	1,200	Cashmere Valley Record	Weekly	NCW Media	1,000	↓	
Chelan	Chelan	Lake Chelan Mirror	Weekly	Prairie Media Inc	2,800	Lake Chelan Mirror	Weekly	NCW Media	3,000		
Leavenworth	Chelan	The Leavenworth Echo	Weekly	Prairie Media Inc	5,450	The Leavenworth Echo	Weekly	NCW Media	1,600	↓	
Port Angeles	Clallam	Peninsula Daily News	Daily	Horvitz Newspapers Inc	17,167	Peninsula Daily News	Daily	Sound Publishing	11,724	↓	
Forks	Clallam	Forks Forum and Peninsula Herald	Weekly	Riesau, Sue Ellen	5,000	Forks Forum	Weekly	Sound Publishing	4,346	↓	
Sequim	Clallam	Sequim Gazette	Weekly	Olympic View Publishing	8,500	Sequim Gazette	Weekly	Sound Publishing	3,835	↓	
Vancouver	Clark	The Columbian	Daily	Columbian Publishing Co	49,488	The Columbian	Daily	Columbian Publishing Co	48,078	↓	
Camas	Clark	Camas-Washougal Post-Record	Weekly	Columbian Publishing Co	10,000	Camas-Washougal Post-Record	Weekly	Columbian Publishing Co	10,000	Constant	
Battle Ground	Clark	The Reflector	Weekly	Case, Marvin	26,700	The Reflector	Weekly	CT Publishing	29,022	↑	
Dayton	Columbia	Dayton Chronicle	Weekly	Touchet Valley News Inc	1,700	Dayton Chronicle	Weekly	2Over Publishing LLC	1,700	Constant	
Longview	Cowlitz	The Daily News	Daily	Lee Enterprises	21,257	The Daily News	Daily	Lee Enterprises	18,536	↓	
East Wenatchee	Douglas	Douglas County Empire Press	Weekly	Cassidy, Donna	1,000	Douglas County Empire Press		Wick Communications (World Publishing)	935	↓	
Republic	Ferry	Republic News Miner	Weekly	Graham Gina M	2,100	Republic News Miner		Graham Gina M			Closed 2016
						Ferry County View		Greg Sheffield	1,250		New
Kennewick	Franklin	Tri-City Herald	Daily	McClatchy	41,666	Tri-City Herald	Daily	Chatham Asset Management	25,663	↓	
Connell	Franklin	Franklin County Graphic	Weekly	Valdez Kathy	3,000	Franklin County Graphic	Weekly	Valdez Kathy	3,000		
Pomeroy	Garfield	East Washingtonian	Weekly	Tom Michael and Teresa M	1,550	East Washingtonian	Weekly	2Over Publishing LLC	800	↓	
Moses Lake	Grant	Columbia Basin Herald	Daily	Hagadone Corporation	8,400	Columbia Basin Herald	Daily	Hagadone Corporation	7,780	↓	
Ephrata	Grant	Grant County Journal	Weekly	Journal Inc	12,774	Grant County Journal	Weekly	Fletcher Jeff	26,792	↑	
Coulee City	Grant	News and Standard	Weekly	Maes ShirleyRae	800	News and Standard		Maes ShirleyRae			Closed
Quincy	Grant	The Quincy Valley Post-Register	Weekly	Kady, Jim	1,890	The Quincy Valley Post-Register	Weekly	Wick Communications (World Publishing)	2,050	↑	
Royal City	Grant	The South County Sun	Weekly	Leitz Lisa and Phillip	800	The South County Sun		Leitz Lisa and Phillip			Closed 2010
Grand Coulee	Grant	The Star	Weekly	Star Publishing Inc.	2,030	The Star	Weekly	Star Publishing Inc.	4,720	↑	
Aberdeen	Grays Harbor	The Daily World	Daily	Stephens Media Group	14,151	The Daily World	Daily	Sound Publishing	6,281	↓	
Ocean Shores	Grays Harbor	North Coast News	Weekly	North Beach Media Inc.	2,010	North Coast News		Sound Publishing			Closed 2021
Westport	Grays Harbor	South Beach Bulletin	Weekly	Stephens Media Group	5,500	South Beach Bulletin		Sound Publishing			Closed 2020
Montesano	Grays Harbor	The Vidette	Weekly	Stephens Media Group	3,800	The Vidette		Sound Publishing			Closed 2021
Coupeville	Island	South Whidbey Record	Weekly	Saylors, Melissa	5,500	South Whidbey Record	Weekly	Sound Publishing	2,374	↓	
Coupeville	Island	Whidbey News Times	Weekly	Sound Publishing	8,800	Whidbey News Times	2x/W	Sound Publishing	3,116	↓	
Coupeville	Island	Coupeville Examiner	Weekly	Doody Mary Kay	1,100	Coupeville Examiner		Doody Mary Kay			Closed 2007

2004						2022					
City	County	Newspaper	Daily/ Weekly	Owner	Circulation	Newspaper	Daily/ Weekly	Owner	Circulation	Increase/ Decrease	Notes
Whidbey	Island	Whidbey Examiner	Weekly	Sound Publishing	1,609	Whidbey Examiner		Sound Publishing			Closed 2017
Port Townsend	Jefferson	The Port Townsend & Jefferson County Leader	Weekly	Wilson Scott	9,000	The Port Townsend & Jefferson County Leader	Weekly	Jefferson County Publications LLC	7,065	↓	
Kent	King	Kent Reporter	Daily	Horvitz Newspapers Inc	42,042	Kent Reporter	Weekly	Sound Publishing	22,810		Daily to Weekly
Seattle	King	The Seattle Times	Daily	Seattle Times Company	231,051	The Seattle Times	Daily	Seattle Times Company	210,156	↓	
Kent	King	King County Journal	Daily	Peter Horvitz	60,000	King County Journal		Purchased by Sound in 2006			Closed 2007
Ballard	King	Ballard News-Tribune	Weekly	Robinson Newspapers Inc.	7,558	Westside Seattle/Ballard News-Tribune	Weekly	Online only; closed print	9,500	↑	
Seattle	King	Seattle Post-Intelligencer	Daily	Hearst Corporation	136,771	Seattle Post-Intelligencer		Hearst Corporation			Closed 2009
Seattle	King	Capitol Hill Times	Weekly	Pacific Publishing Co	16,000	Capitol Hill Times		RIM Publications			Closed 2020
Seattle	King	The Facts News	Weekly	Beaver, Dennis	15,000	The Facts News	Weekly	Marla Beaver	50,000	↑	
Federal Way	King	Federal Way Mirror	Weekly	Sound Publishing	30,516	Federal Way Mirror	Weekly	Sound Publishing	28,756	↓	
Issaquah	King	New Castle News	Weekly	Issaquah Press/Seattle Times		New Castle News		Seattle Times Company			Closed 2017
						Issaquah Reporter	Weekly	Online only -- Sound Publishing	30,111		New
Kirkland	King	Kirkland Reporter	Weekly	Sound Publishing	25,205	Kirkland Reporter	Weekly	Online only -- Sound Publishing	22,684	↓	
Mercer Island	King	Mercer Island Reporter	Weekly	Horvitz Newspapers Inc	5,000	Mercer Island Reporter	Weekly	Sound Publishing	2,658	↓	
Seattle	King	Queen Anne & Magnolia News	Weekly	Pacific Publishing Co	19,800	Queen Anne & Magnolia News	Weekly	Pacific Publishing	5,000	↓	
Kirkland	King	Redmond Reporter	Weekly	Sound Publishing	22,537	Redmond Reporter	Weekly	Online only -- Sound Publishing	19,782	↓	
Seattle	King	The Seattle Medium	Weekly	Owens, Joan and Bennett, Chris B.	13,500	The Seattle Medium	Weekly	Tiloben Publishing Co. Inc.	13,500	Constant	
Federal Way	King	Seattle Weekly	Weekly	Quickfish Media Inc	97,195	Seattle Weekly	Weekly	Online only -- Sound Publishing	45,066	↓	
Burien	King	Snoqualmie Valley Record	Weekly	Horbitz, Peter	4,700	Snoqualmie Valley Record	Weekly	Sound Publishing	11,226	↑	
Vashon	King	Vashon-Maury Island Beachcomber	Weekly	Sound Publishing	4,150	Vashon-Maury Island Beachcomber	Weekly	Sound Publishing	2,594	↓	
Maple Valley	King	Voice of the Valley	Weekly	Voice of The Valley	16,100	Voice of the Valley	Weekly	Online only/Donna Hayes, Owner/publisher	17,500	↑	
Seattle	King	West Seattle Herald	Weekly	Robinson Newspapers Inc.	11,500	West Seattle Herald	Weekly	Online only -- Robinson Newspapers Inc.	12,000	↑	
Woodinville	King	The Woodinville Weekly	Weekly	Edwards Carol	32,200	The Woodinville Weekly	Weekly	EastSide Media Corporation	18,600	↓	
Kent	King	Auburn Reporter	Weekly	Sound Publishing	24,384	Auburn Reporter	Weekly	Sound Publishing	20,038	↓	
Kent	King	Renton Reporter	Weekly	Sound Publishing	25,682	Renton Reporter	Weekly	Online only -- Sound Publishing	21,888	↓	
Burien	King	Highline Times	Weekly	Robinson Newspapers Inc.	20,000	Westside Seattle/Highline Times	Weekly	Online only -- Robinson Newspapers	10,000	↓	
Issaquah	King	Sammamish Review	Weekly	Seattle Times Company	15,000	Sammamish Review		Seattle Times Company			Closed 2017
Shoreline	King	Shoreline Enterprise	Weekly	Washington Post Company	24,600	Shoreline Enterprise		Washington Post Company			Closed 2002
						Bellevue Reporter	Weekly	Online only -- Sound Publishing	30,203		New
Seattle	King	The Stranger	Weekly	Keck, Tim	83,023	The Stranger	Weekly	In transition print operation closed 2020		Unknown	

Back to Table of Contents
Back to study

2004						2022					
City	County	Newspaper	Daily/ Weekly	Owner	Circulation	Newspaper	Daily/ Weekly	Owner	Circulation	Increase/ Decrease	Notes
Federal Way	King	Federal Way News	Weekly	Hollings Roger	15,046	Federal Way News		Sound Publishing			Closed 2009
						Issaquah-Sammamish Reporter	Weekly	Sound Publishing			New
Enumclaw	King	The Enumclaw Courier-Herald	Weekly	Courier-Herald	6,800	The Courier Herald	Weekly	Sound Publishing		Merged with Pierce County papers	
	King	SnoVallley started in 2008				SnoValley Star		Seattle Times Co.			Closed 2017
Issaquah	King	The Issaquah Press	Weekly	Seattle Times Company	19,200	The Issaquah Press		Seattle Times Co.			Closed 2017
						Covington-Maple Valley Reporter	Weekly	Online only -- Sound Publishing	22,650		New
	King	Beacon Hill News/South District Journal	Weekly	Pacific Publishing Co	11,000	Beacon Hill News		Pacific Publishing			Closed 2008
	King	North Seattle Herald-Outlook	Weekly	Pacific Publishing Co	8,000	North Seattle Herald Outlook		Pacific Publishing			Closed 2012
Bremerton	Kitsap	Kitsap Sun	Daily	EW Scripps	30,332	Kitsap Sun	Daily	Gannett	16,683	↓	
Bainbridge Island	Kitsap	Bainbridge Island Review	Weekly	Sound Publishing	4,602	Bainbridge Island Review	Weekly	Sound Publishing	1,982	↓	
Poulsbo	Kitsap	Central Kitsap Reporter	Weekly	Sound Publishing	21,000	Central Kitsap Reporter		Sound Publishing			Closed 2021
Poulsbo	Kitsap	North Kitsap Herald	Weekly	Sound Publishing	1,500	Kitsap Daily News	Weekly	Sound Publishing	10,092	↑	
Port Orchard	Kitsap	Port Orchard Independent	Weekly	Sound Publishing	16,000	Port Orchard Independent	Weekly	Sound Publishing	1,353	↓	
Bremerton	Kitsap	Bremerton Patriot	Weekly	Sound Publishing	12,200	Bremerton Patriot	Weekly	Sound Publishing			Closed 2017
Ellensburg	Kittitas	Daily Record	Daily	Pioneer News Group	5,500	Daily Record	Daily	Adams Publishing Group	5,523	↑	
Cle Elum	Kittitas	Northern Kittitas County Tribune	Weekly	Oahe Publishing Corp.	3,800	Northern Kittitas County Tribune	Weekly	Oahe Publishing Corp	3,000	↓	
White Salmon	Klickitat	Enterprise	Weekly	Eagle Newspapers Inc	2,725	Enterprise	Weekly	Columbia Gorge News	2,500	↓	
Goldendale	Klickitat	The Goldendale Sentinel	Weekly	McNab, Andy	3,350	The Goldendale Sentinel	Weekly	Tartan Publications	3,200	↓	
Centralia	Lewis	The Chronicle	Daily	Lafromboise Communications Inc	14,060	The Chronicle	Daily	CT Publishing	10,200	↓	
Winlock	Lewis	Lewis County News	Weekly		9,000	Lewis County News	Weekly	Online only -- Flannery Publications	6,500	↓	
Davenport	Lincoln	Davenport Times	Weekly	Journal Newspapers Inc	2,243	Davenport Times	Weekly	Free Press Publishing	2,200	↓	
Odessa	Lincoln	The Odessa Record	Weekly	Walter, Don	1,250	The Odessa Record	Weekly	Free Press Publishing	1,250	Constant	
Wilbur	Lincoln	The Wilbur Register	Weekly	Stedman Frank	1,646	The Wilbur Register	Weekly	Stedman Frank	1,200	↓	
Shelton	Mason	Shelton-Mason County Journal	Weekly	Shelton Publishing	9,407	Shelton-Mason County Journal	Weekly	John Lester, publisher/Mullen Newspaper	7,200	↓	
Brewster	Okanogan	Brewster Quad City Herald	Weekly	Vallance, Ike	2,600	Brewster Quad City Herald	Weekly	NCW Media	2,522	↓	
Twisp	Okanogan	Methow Valley News	Weekly	Methow Valley Publishing	3,535	Methow Valley News	Weekly	Methow Valley Publishing	3,035	↓	
Oroville	Okanogan	Okanogan Valley Gazette-Tribune	Weekly	Prairie Media Inc	2,600	Okanogan Valley Gazette-Tribune	Weekly	Sound Publishing	1,402	↓	
Omak	Okanogan	The Omak-Okanogan County Chronicle	Weekly	Eagle Newspapers Inc	2,500	The Omak-Okanogan County Chronicle	Weekly	Teresa Myers, Publisher/Mullen Newspaper	6,900	↑	
Long Beach	Pacific	Chinook Observer	Weekly	East Oregonian Publishing Company	6,500	Chinook Observer	Weekly	East Oregonian Publishing Company	6,800	↑	
Raymond	Pacific	Willapa Harbor Herald	Weekly	Flannery Publications	23,200	Willapa Harbor Herald	Weekly	Flannery Publications	5,141	↓	
Newport	Pend Oreille	The Newport Miner	Weekly	Willenbrock Fred	3,800	The Newport Miner	Weekly	Michelle Nedved / Mullen Newspaper	1,700	↓	
Tacoma	Pierce	Tacoma Weekly	Weekly	Unknown	Unknown	Tacoma Weekly	Weekly	Pierce County Community Newspaper Group	24,000	Unknown	

| 2004 | | | | | | 2022 | | | | | |
City	County	Newspaper	Daily/ Weekly	Owner	Circulation	Newspaper	Daily/ Weekly	Owner	Circulation	Increase/ Decrease	Notes
Tacoma	Pierce	The News Tribune	Daily	McClatchy	127,928	The News Tribune	Daily	Chatham Asset Management	54,000	↓	
Gig Harbor	Pierce	The Peninsula Gateway	Weekly	McClatchy	9,500	The Peninsula Gateway	Weekly	Chatham Asset Management	4,993	↓	
Puyallup	Pierce	Pierce County Herald/Herald Sampler	Weekly	Iverson Lynn	40,000	Pierce County Herald		Iverson Lynn			Closed
Puyallup	Pierce	Puyallup Herald	Weekly	McClatchy	21,900	Puyallup Herald	Weekly	Chatham Asset Management	27,000	↑	
Eatonville	Pierce	The South Pierce County Dispatch	Weekly	Ringtree Inc	20,000	The South Pierce County Dispatch	Weekly	Ringtree Inc	1,200	↓	Online only
Tacoma	Pierce	The Tacoma True Citizen	Weekly	Owens, Joan and Bennett, Chris B.	10,000	The Tacoma True Citizen	Weekly	Bennett, Chris B.	10,000	Constant	
Eastsound	San Juan	The Islands' Sounder	Weekly	Sound Publishing	3,500	The Islands' Sounder	Weekly	Sound Publishing	1,197	↓	
Lopez Island	San Juan	The Islands' Weekly	Weekly	Sound Publishing	8,500	The Islands' Weekly	Weekly	Sound Publishing	1,892	↓	
Friday Harbor	San Juan	The Journal of the San Juan Islands	Weekly	Sound Publishing	4,851	The Journal of the San Juan Islands	Weekly	Sound Publishing	898	↓	
Mount Vernon	Skagit	Skagit Valley Herald	Daily	Pioneer News Group	17,384	Skagit Valley Herald	Daily	Adams Publishing Group	13,942	↓	
Anacortes	Skagit	Anacortes American	Weekly	Pioneer News Group	4,531	Anacortes American	Weekly	Adams Publishing Group	3,276	↓	
Mount Vernon	Skagit	Argus	Weekly	Pioneer News Group	9,000	Argus		Pioneer News Group			Closed/See GoSkagit.com
Sedro-Woolley	Skagit	Courier-Times	Weekly	Pioneer News Group	6,000	Courier-Times		Pioneer News Group			
La Conner	Skagit	La Conner Weekly News	Weekly	Pentz Andy	1,915	La Conner Weekly News	Weekly	Ken Stern	1,550	↓	
Stevenson	Skamania	Skamania County Pioneer	Weekly	Diehl, Patricia	2,600	Skamania County Pioneer	Weekly	DeVaul Publishing	2,600	Constant	
Everett	Snohomish	The Daily Herald	Daily	Washington Post Company	50,320	The Daily Herald	Daily	Sound Publishing	33,543	↓	
						North County Outlook	Weekly	Sue Stevenson	10,000		New
Marysville	Snohomish	The Arlington Times	Weekly	Sun News Inc	9,000	The Arlington Times		Sun News Inc			Closed 2020
Bothell	Snohomish	Bothell-Kenmore Reporter	Weekly	King County Journal Newspapers	28,000	Bothell-Kenmore Reporter	2x/ month	Sound Publishing	21,341	↓	
Mukilteo	Snohomish	Edmonds Beacon	Weekly	Archipley Paul	10,000	Edmonds Beacon	Weekly	Beacon Publishing Inc.	10,100	↑	
Edmonds	Snohomish	Edmonds Enterprise	Weekly	Washington Post Company	18,000	Edmonds Enterprise		Absorbed by Weekly Herald			Closed 2012
Everett	Snohomish	Everett News	Weekly	Mack Dave	49,000	Everett News		Mack Dave			Closed
Lake Stevens	Snohomish	Lake Stevens Journal	Weekly	Cahoon Desiree	17,487	Lake Stevens Journal		Cahoon Desiree			Closed
Lynwood	Snohomish	Lynnwood Enterprise	Weekly	Washington Post Company	26,500	Lynnwood Enterprise		Absorbed by Weekly Herald			Closed 2012
Marysville	Snohomish	Marysville Globe	Weekly	Sun News Inc	12,782	Marysville Globe		Sound Publishing			Closed 2021
Mill Creek	Snohomish	Mill Creek Enterprise	Weekly	Washington Post Company	10,950	Mill Creek Enterprise		Absorbed by Weekly Herald			Closed 2012
Monroe	Snohomish	Monroe Monitor and Valley News	Weekly	Robinson, Ken	4,000	Monroe Monitor and Valley News		Pacific Publishing			Closed 2021
Mukilteo	Snohomish	Mukilteo Beacon	Weekly	Archipley Paul	9,000	Mukilteo Beacon	Weekly	Beacon Publishing Inc.	10,166	↑	
Snohomish	Snohomish	Snohomish County Tribune	Weekly	Mack Dave	35,000	Snohomish County Tribune	Weekly	Pacific Publishing	2,100	↓	
Stanwood	Snohomish	Stanwood/Camano News	Weekly	Pinkham Dave	16,000	Stanwood/Camano News	Weekly	Adams Publishing Group	4,000	↓	
Edmonds	Snohomish	The Weekly Herald	Weekly	Sound Publishing	51,084	The Weekly Herald		Sound Publishing			Closed 2012
						Lynnwood Times	Bi-W	Mario Lotmore	10,000		New
Spokane	Spokane	The Spokesman-Review	Daily	Cowles Publishing Co	99,002	The Spokesman-Review	Daily	Cowles Publishing Co	56,629	↓	
Cheney	Spokane	Cheney Free Press	Weekly	Journal Communications Inc	44,017	Cheney Free Press	Weekly	Free Press Publishing	3,695	↓	
Deer Park	Spokane	Deer Park Tribune	Weekly	Horizon Publications	10,500	Deer Park Tribune	Weekly	Horizon Publications	12,004	↑	
Spokane	Spokane	Pacific Northwest Inlander	Weekly	Inland Publications	45,000	Pacific Northwest Inlander	Weekly	McGregor, Ted	52,050	↑	
Spokane Valley	Spokane	Spokane Valley News Herald	Weekly	Cheney Free Press	11,000	Spokane Valley News Herald	Weekly	Free Press Publishing	5,500	↓	
Chewelah	Stevens	The Independent	Weekly	Blake, Nancy	2,350	The Independent	Weekly	Chewelah Independent	100	↓	
Colville	Stevens	Statesman-Examiner	Weekly	Horizon Publications	4,607	Statesman-Examiner	Weekly	Horizon Publications	4,365	↓	
Olympia	Thurston	The Olympian	Daily	Gannett	33,848	The Olympian	Daily	Chatham Asset Management	17,401	↓	

| 2004 | | | | | | 2022 | | | | | |
City	County	Newspaper	Daily/ Weekly	Owner	Circulation	Newspaper	Daily/ Weekly	Owner	Circulation	Increase/ Decrease	Notes
Yelm	Thurston	Nisqually Valley News	Weekly	Lafromboise Communications Inc	24,000	Nisqually Valley News	Weekly	CT Publishing	4,000	↓	
Tenino	Thurston	The Tenino Independent	Weekly	DeVaul Publishing Inc	1,200	The Tenino Independent	Weekly	DeVaul Publishing	1,200	Constant	
Cathlamet	Wahkiakum	The Wahkiakum County Eagle	Weekly	Nelson, Bob	1,728	The Wahkiakum County Eagle	Weekly	Rick Nelson	1,693	↓	
Walla Walla	Walla Walla	Walla Walla Union-Bulletin	Daily	Seattle Times Company	14,274	Walla Walla Union-Bulletin	Daily	Seattle Times Company	11,731	↓	
Waitsburg	Walla Walla	The Waitsburg Times	Weekly	Baker, Cathy	1,400	The Waitsburg Times	Weekly	Lane Gwinn, Publisher	1,600	↑	
Bellingham	Whatcom	The Bellingham Herald	Daily	Gannett	23,938	The Bellingham Herald	Daily	Chatham Asset Management	13,073	↓	
Blaine	Whatcom	The Northern Light	Weekly	Point Roberts Press Inc	9,000	The Northern Light	Weekly	Point Roberts Press Inc.	10,486	↑	
Ferndale	Whatcom	Record-Journal	Weekly	Lewis Publishing Company Inc.	7,100	Ferndale Record	Weekly	Lewis Publishing Company Inc.	6,950	↓	
Lynden	Whatcom	Lynden Tribune	Weekly	Lewis Publishing Company Inc.	14,000	Lynden Tribune	Weekly	Lewis Publishing Company Inc.	12,250	↓	
						Cascadia Daily News	Daily	David Syre			New Jan. 2022
Colfax	Whitman	Whitman County Gazette	Weekly	Lewiston Tribune	4,430	Whitman County Gazette	Weekly	Free Press Publishing	3,802	↓	
Sunnyside	Yakima	Daily Sun-News	Daily	Eagle Newspapers Inc	3,887	Daily Sun-News		Eagle Newspapers Inc			Closed
						Sunnyside Sun	Weekly	Andy McNab, publisher	3,818		New, replaces Daily Sun-News
Yakima	Yakima	Yakima Herald-Republic	Daily	Seattle Times Company	38,104	Yakima Herald-Republic	Daily	Seattle Times Company	24,827	↓	
Grandview	Yakima	The Grandview Herald	Weekly	Fournier Newspapers	2,481	The Grandview Herald	Weekly	Valley Publishing Company	1,500	↓	
Toppenish	Yakima	Review Independent	Weekly	Flint Journal	6,800	Review Independent		Lindsey, Mike & Pat			Closed
Wapato	Yakima	Wapato Independent	Weekly	Flint Publishing	2,000	Wapato Independent		Flint Publishing			Closed in 2006

2004 Quick Stats
Number of daily papers: 23
Number of weekly papers: 120
Total number of newspapers: 143

2022 Quick Stats
Number of daily papers: 20
Number of weekly papers: 96
Total number of newspapers: 116

What Changed?
Closures: 37
New papers opened: 10
Circulation decreases: 73

*All Sound Publishing circulation numbers come from the company website.
** Kent Reporter is a merger of Kent Reporter, Covington, Black Diamond, Maple Valley Reporter papers.
*** The Whidbey News Times prints jointly with the South Whidbey Record on Wednesdays.

Sources include the Washington State Library; "Chronicling America" from the U.S. Library of Congress; SoundPublishing.com; the Washington Newspaper Publishers Association; Allied Daily Newspapers of Washington; Penelope Abernathy's studies at the University of North Carolina's Hussman School of Journalism and Media; individual newspaper websites; individual publishers' websites; Wikipedia; MondoTimes.com

Cascadia Daily News comes to town

In downtown Bellingham, a nearly 100-year-old building that once housed the headquarters of Puget Sound Power and Light and later served as a bus depot is now home to a new publication whose owners promise to keep residents informed about what's happening in their community.

The **Cascadia Daily News** - founded by two men with deep Bellingham roots — occupies two large offices on the top floor of the three-story building. Despite an exodus of businesses to a mall that opened in 1988 north of the city center, the Art Deco-style building, constructed in 1930, has been maintained over the years. Today it also features a restaurant and other offices.

Artist and entrepreneur David Syre, a fourth-generation Whatcom County resident, and former Seattle Times journalist Ron Judd, who has lived in Bellingham for more than 20 years, are at the helm of the Daily News, which launched in January 2022. Syre is the owner/publisher and Judd is executive editor. The two launched the Cascadia operation after Chatham Asset Management purchased The Bellingham Herald in a bankruptcy sale from McClatchy Newspapers. The Herald has seen dramatic declines in content over recent years.

"Community journalism — the kind that reports on the lives of our people while also serving as an important check on local government — is sorely needed," Syre wrote in announcing the launch of the Daily News in an earlier publication he owned, Cascadia Weekly.[125] "It has been my goal to return locally owned and independently operated daily journalism to the people here," added Syre, 80.

With a staff of nine — a mix of veteran and less experienced journalists — plus Judd and four interns, the Daily News publishes a daily online edition and a weekly print edition. The print edition — 24 pages, three sections — features significant stories from the preceding week with coverage of local government and business, high school and college sports, recreation, arts and entertainment, and health.

Photo by Jack Carver, 1953
Whatcom Museum #1995.1.7790

The Cascadia Daily News building once was a bus depot. Credit: Jack Carver, Whatcom Museum

In an interview with the news study committee, Judd emphasized that local journalism is important to the community. He recalled a Bellingham general election in 2015 when five open city council seats were uncontested. "To me that is a sign of neglect by local media and local process," Judd said.

Ron Judd, left, and David Syre

At present, both the digital and print editions, underwritten by Syre, are free. Judd said the goal is for subscriptions and advertising to cover the costs. He said small, independent businesses will prefer advertising in a local publication over sites maintained by the tech giants. Furthermore, he said, print ads are more effective than online ads.

Judd said that the Daily News has met with enthusiastic community support. "The public sees the need for this. They know they aren't necessarily informed," he said.

Back to Table of Contents
Back to study

Newspapers by county

Newspapers by County

Figure 20

County	Population	Paper	Daily/ Weekly	Circulation	Notes
Adams	20,274	Ritzville Adams County Journal	Weekly	2,146	
Asotin	22,480	Lewiston Tribune	Daily		Published in Lewiston, Idaho, covers Asotin County
Benton	213,702	Prosser Record-Bulletin	Weekly	2,809	
Chelan	78,544	Cashmere Valley Record	Weekly	1,000	
		Lake Chelan Mirror	Weekly	3,000	
		Leavenworth Echo	Weekly	1,600	
		The Wenatchee World	Daily	15,001	
Clallam	79,671	Forks Forum	Weekly	4,346	
		Peninsula Daily News	Daily	11,724	
		Sequim Gazette	Weekly	3,835	
Clark	508,683	Camas-Washougal Post Record	Weekly	10,000	
		The Columbian	Daily	48,078	
		The Reflector	Weekly	29,022	
Columbia	3,823	Dayton Chronicle	Weekly	1,700	
Cowlitz	116,116	The Daily News	Daily	18,536	
Douglas	45,469	Douglas County Empire Press	Weekly	935	
Ferry	7,594	Ferry County View	Weekly	1,250	
Franklin	98,879	Franklin County Graphic	Weekly	3,000	
		The Tri-City Herald	Daily	25,663	
Garfield	2,180	East Washingtonian	Weekly	800	

County	Population	Paper	Daily/Weekly	Circulation	Notes
Grant	100,916	Columbia Basin Herald	Daily	7,780	
		Grant County Journal	Weekly	26,792	
		Quincy Valley Post/Register	Weekly	2,050	
		The Star	Weekly	4,720	
Grays Harbor	78,841	Daily World	Daily	6,281	
Island	87,883	South Whidbey Record	Weekly	2,374	
		Whidbey News Times	Weekly	3,116	
Jefferson	33,646	Port Townsend & Jefferson County Leader	Weekly	7,065	
King	2,326,036	Auburn Reporter	Weekly	20,038	
		Bellevue Reporter	Weekly	30,203	
		Covington/Maple Valley Reporter	Weekly	22,650	
		Federal Way Mirror	Weekly	28,756	
		Issaquah Reporter	Weekly	30,111	
		Kent Reporter	Weekly	22,810	
		Kirkland Reporter	Weekly	22,684	
		Mercer Island Reporter	Weekly	2,658	
		Queen Anne & Magnolia News	Weekly	5,000	
		Redmond Reporter	Weekly	19,782	
		Renton Reporter	Weekly	21,888	
		Seattle Medium	Weekly	13,500	
		Seattle Times	Daily	210,156	
		Seattle Weekly	Weekly	45,066	
		Snoqualmie Valley Record	Weekly	11,226	
		The Facts News	Weekly	50,000	
		Vashon-Maury Beachcomber	Weekly	2,594	
		Voice of the Valley	Weekly	17,500	
		West Seattle Herald	Weekly	12,000	
		Westside Seattle/Ballard News Tribune	Weekly	9,500	
		Westside Seattle/Highline Times	Weekly	10,000	
		Woodinville Weekly	Weekly	18,600	
Kitsap	278,064	Bainbridge Island Review	Weekly	1,982	
		Kitsap Daily News	Weekly	10,092	
		Kitsap Sun	Daily	16,683	
		Port Orchard Independent	Weekly	1,353	
Kittitas	49,666	Daily Record	Daily	5,523	
		Northern Kittitas County Tribune	Weekly	3,000	
Klickitat	23,292	Enterprise	Weekly	2,500	Published in The Dalles, Oregon
		Goldendale Sentinel	Weekly	3,200	
Lewis	84,121	Lewis County News	Weekly	6,500	
		The Chronicle	Daily	10,200	
Lincoln	11,578	Davenport Times	Weekly	2,200	
		Odessa Record	Weekly	1,250	
		Wilbur Register	Weekly	1,200	
Mason	70,932	Shelton-Mason County Journal	Weekly	7,200	
Okanogan	42,621	Brewster Quad City Herald	Weekly	2,522	
		Methow Valley News	Weekly	3,035	
		Okanogan Valley Gazette-Tribune	Weekly	1,402	
		Omak-Okanogan County Chronicle	Weekly	6,900	
Pacific	23,662	Chinook Observer	Weekly	6,800	
		Willapa Harbor Herald	Weekly	5,141	
Pend Oreille	14,138	Newport Miner	Weekly	1,700	
Pierce	938,652	Dispatch South Pierce County	Weekly	1,200	
		Peninsula Gateway	Weekly	4,993	
		Puyallup Herald	Weekly	27,000	
		Tacoma News Tribune	Daily	54,000	

County	Population	Paper	Daily/ Weekly	Circulation	Notes
		Tacoma True Citizen	Weekly	10,000	
		Tacoma Weekly	Weekly	24,000	
		The Courier-Herald	Weekly	25,392	
San Juan	18,956	Journal of San Juan Island	Weekly	898	
		The Islands' Sounder	Weekly	1,197	
		The Islands' Weekly	Weekly	1,892	
Skagit	133,315	Anacortes American	Weekly	3,276	
		La Conner Weekly News	Weekly	1,550	
		Skagit Valley Herald	Daily	13,942	
Skamania	12,575	Skamania County Pioneer	Weekly	2,600	
Snohomish	849,156	Bothell-Kenmore Reporter	2x / mo.	21,341	
		Edmonds Beacon	Weekly	10,100	
		Lynnwood Times	Bi-Weekly	10,000	
		Mukilteo Beacon	Weekly	10,166	
		North County Outlook	Weekly	10,000	
		Snohomish County Tribune	Weekly	2,100	
		Stanwood Camano News	Weekly	4,000	
		The Herald	Daily	33,543	
Spokane	550,383	Cheney Free Pres	Weekly	3,695	
		Deer Park Tribune	Weekly	12,004	
		Pacific Northwest Inlander	Weekly	52,050	
		Spokane Valley News Herald	Weekly	5,500	
		The Spokesman-Review	Daily	56,629	
Stevens	47,220	Statesman Examiner	Weekly	4,365	
		The Independent	Weekly	100	
Thurston	303,976	Nisqually Valley News	Weekly	4,000	
		The Olympian	Daily	17,401	
		The Tenino Independent	Weekly	1,200	
Wahkiakum	4,707	Wahkiakum County Eagle	Weekly	1,693	
Walla Walla	61,195	Waitsburg Times	Weekly	1,600	
		Walla Walla Union-Bulletin	Daily	11,731	
Whatcom	241,397	Bellingham Herald	Daily	13,073	
		Cascadia Daily News	Daily		Launched February 2022
		Ferndale Record	Weekly	6,950	
		Lynden Tribune	Weekly	12,250	
		Northern Light	Weekly	10,486	
Whitman	51,367	Moscow-Pullman Daily News	Daily	7,400	Published Moscow, Idaho
		Whitman County Gazette	Weekly	3,802	
Yakima	251,806	Grandview Herald	Weekly	1,500	
		Sunnyside Sun	Weekly	3,818	
		The Yakima Herald-Republic	Daily	24,827	

2022 population figures from: World Population Review. Population of Counties in Washington (2022). Retrieved Feb 26, 2022, from https://worldpopulationreview.com/us-counties/states/wa. Additional assistance from Municipal Research and Services Center of Washington.

Newspaper circulation information from the Library of Congress Chronicling America; Washington State Library Newspaper Database; Penny Abernathy, Northwestern University; Washington Newspaper Publishers Association, Fred Obee; Allied Daily Newspapers of Washington, Rowland Thompson; and with supplemental circulation information from Mondotimes.com.

Back to Table of Contents
Back to study

Sound Publishing newspapers

Newspaper	Frequency	Circulation	Increase/ Decrease	Notes
Auburn Reporter	Weekly	20,038	↓	
Bainbridge Island Review	Weekly	1,982	↓	
Bellevue Reporter	Weekly	30,203	**New**	Online only
Bothell-Kenmore Reporter	2x/Mo.	21,341	↓	
Covington-Maple Valley Reporter	Weekly	22,650	**New**	Online only
Federal Way Mirror	Weekly	28,756	↓	
Forks Forum	Weekly	4,346	↓	
Issaquah Reporter	Weekly	30,111	**New**	Online only
Issaquah-Sammamish Reporter	Weekly		**New**	Online only
Kent Reporter*	Weekly	22,810	↓	Daily to Weekly
Kirkland Reporter	Weekly	22,684	↓	Online only
Kitsap Daily News	Weekly	10,092	↑	
Mercer Island Reporter	Weekly	2,658	↓	
Okanogan Valley Gazette-Tribune	Weekly	1,402	↓	
Peninsula Daily News	Daily	11,724	↓	
Port Orchard Independent	Weekly	1,353	↓	
Redmond Reporter	Weekly	19,782	↓	Online only
Renton Reporter	Weekly	21,888	↓	Online only
Seattle Weekly	Weekly	45,066	↓	Online only
Sequim Gazette	Weekly	3,835	↓	
Snoqualmie Valley Record	Weekly	11,226	↑	
South Whidbey Record	Weekly	2,374	↓	
The Courier Herald	Weekly	**Merged with Pierce County papers**		
The Daily Herald	Daily	33,543	↓	
The Daily World	Daily	6,281	↓	
The Islands' Sounder	Weekly	1,197	↓	
The Islands' Weekly	Weekly	1,892	↓	
The Journal of the San Juan Islands	Weekly	898	↓	
Vashon-Maury Island Beachcomber	Weekly	2,594	↓	
Whidbey News Times	2x/Wk.	3,116	↓	

Figure 21 - Sound Publishing is owned by Black Press Media, a Canadian corporation that also owns newspapers in British Columbia and Alberta.

Back to Table of Contents
Back to study

Observer offers meaty coverage

With the state's longest sandy beach, plenty of tasty seafood, a bustling boardwalk, a plethora of art shows and miles of hiking, Washington's southwest coast is, for many, a vacationer's wonderland.

Some might be surprised to learn the area also is home to an award-winning newspaper that packs a punch. The weekly **Chinook Observer** consistently tracks the goings-on of local government, providing its 5,000 subscribers with solid coverage and meaningful hard news.

"We do everything we absolutely can each week to give people a really good, meaty product," editor/publisher Matt Winters told the news study committee during a July 2022 interview. "We're constantly looking at four incorporated cities. Raymond is the biggest and we focus on Ilwaco and Long Beach and there's county government in South Bend."

The Chinook Observer staff first worked in this shed in the town of Chinook before building its own headquarters in 1905. Pictured are staff and some members of the Chinook community on July 4, 1903. George Hibbert, seated, left, was one of the Observer's founders. Credit: Chinook Observer.

Case in point is the Observer's extensive coverage of U.S. Immigration and Customs Enforcement activities and immigration issues throughout the Long Beach peninsula region. For its dogged reporting, the Washington Newspaper Publishers Association recognized the more than 100-year-old weekly with its statewide Public Service Award in 2018. The Observer has garnered scores of other statewide general excellence awards over the years as well.

Winters, who earned a law degree from the University of Wyoming but opted for a journalism career, said the Observer's commitment to accountable journalism is, at least partly, the reason the paper has succeeded while other papers have struggled.

The Observer's success, he said, is also due to the fact that it is published by EO Media, a longtime family-owned company with 17 newspapers to its name and a robust commitment to community support for the news. "Family ownership is the biggest contributor to the Observer being as strong as it is," Winters said.

That's not to suggest the paper hasn't had challenges. Winter noted that its staff now is much smaller, with five full-timers including himself, compared with 20 years ago, when the staff numbered a dozen.

For instance, in 2000, when the paper celebrated its centennial, the staff included a full-time photographer. "We phased that out 10 years ago. We expect people to write and take photos," Winters said.

The company has also centralized some operations, including, for instance, display advertising design, which now takes place across the border and the Columbia River, in Astoria, Oregon. Other functions happen in Bend, Oregon, too.

Matt Winters

With increased paper costs, leadership also opted to reduce the dimensions of the print edition and the page count. Twenty years ago, during the summer, when tourism is the highest, it wasn't unusual to publish a 30-page edition. "Now, routinely, 20 is a more typical count," the editor said.

Winters said a reduction in ad sales means the Observer relies more on circulation as a revenue source, prompting him in June 2022 to increase the price of a single copy from $2 to $2.50. And the paper's online paywall, fully implemented within the last five years, generates revenue.

Circulation is strong and is actually up with the pandemic. Winters said that the region's population, mostly stagnant at least since his 1992 arrival, started growing in 2020. "It has really expanded and we've seen a 10% growth in circulation."

Pacific County, he said, is the state's 10th fastest growing county. Winters said the print and digital subscriptions for the Observer were up 17% from 2020 to 2022.

Back to Table of Contents
Back to study

Craigslist, "newspaper killer"

Most people who talk about the decline of newspapers say it was caused by the collapse of advertising as a primary financing source. The push over the cliff of newspaper solvency started in 1995 with an email list of friends created by Craig Newmark in San Francisco.

Within 15 years, the free online classified ad service named Craigslist had become wildly successful, available in 70 countries, and worth $100 million. During the same time period, newspaper classified revenue dropped 70%, from $19 billion to $6 billion. New York Magazine called Newmark "The Exploder of Journalism," and others referred to Craigslist as "newspaper killer."

Classified ads made up as much as half of newspaper advertising revenue in 2000. Classified ads are small, text-only ads used for such purposes as renting apartments, finding lost dogs, and reselling refrigerators.

A 2013 study of Craigslist's impact on newspapers showed that when the service appeared in a market where the local newspaper carried a substantial number of classified ads, the newspaper lost classified ad sales, cut the price of display ads, raised subscription prices, and suffered shrinking circulation.

People placing classified ads saved up to $5 billion during 2000 to 2007 because of Craigslist, the study said. Craigslist postings are free, except for job and apartment listings in major cities, dealer car, truck, and furniture listings, and service listings. Newmark said he started his service because "we are just trying to give people a break."

Newmark has given back to the journalism community over the years, most recently a $20 million donation in 2018 to the City University of New York graduate school of journalism foundation. The CUNY board of trustees named the school in his honor.

Newmark in 2017 gave the CUNY journalism school $1.5 million for its News Integrity Initiative to help fight fake news, and the school raised another $14 million for the effort.

Among other organizations Newmark has helped are the Columbia Journalism Review, Poynter Institute for Media Studies, ProPublica, and the Sunlight Foundation.

But like so many other businesses, Craigslist has been affected by the rise of social media sites such as Facebook Marketplace, Nextdoor, and others. In 2020, Craigslist revenue dropped by 26%, according to AIM Group. Although traffic is still in the top 25 for U.S. websites, it's only about 40% of what it was in 2017.

Back to Table of Contents
Back to study

Media literacy: Learning what's credible

The decline in local news may have one elusive cause: the public's lack of tools to discern the credibility of the media messages that bombard them daily.

Any college educator who's taught a media literacy course in the United States during the past 20 years has heard students lament. "Why are we just learning this now?" they cry.

Students' frustration stems from a lack of instruction about media in their early education. They know how to use social media, but they have little notion of how these platforms may affect their values or behaviors.

One long-term solution to the decline in local news may be media literacy education: educating students as early as possible how to spot misinformation and to understand how reliable local news is essential to democracy.

Media literacy originally was proposed abroad in the 1970s, to protect much of the rest of the developed world from the proliferation of U.S. movies and television. For more than 50 years, many democracies in Europe, Canada, and Australia have provided young people with the tools they need to evaluate the validity of content. These countries and others have made media education compulsory in early grades.

As educators have spoken out about the need for media/news education, some state legislators have listened. A 2020 report from Media Literacy NOW cites 14 U.S. states, including Washington, that have introduced and passed legislation to implement media literacy language into their public school curriculum.

Washington's law, passed in 2016, focuses specifically on digital citizenship, internet safety, and media literacy and is revisited by the Legislature every year.

Proponents of media literacy do not tout it as a panacea to boost local news today, but this education may provide a process to help local news operations regain an audience that appreciates the value of their product.

Back to Table of Contents
Back to study

Media Literacy tools

Fact checking

Media bias/fact check:
   https://mediabiasfactcheck.com
Poynter Fact-checking Network:
   https://www.poynter.org/ifcn/
   https://www.politifact.com/
Annenburg Public Policy Center:
   https://www.factcheck.org/
Snopes:
   https://www.snopes.com
Washington Post fact-checker
   https://www.washingtonpost.com/news/fact-checker/
Media bias chart:
   https://www.allsides.com/media-bias/media-bias-chart

Disinformation

Tools that fight disinformation online - RAND Corp:
   https://www.rand.org/research/projects/truth-decay/fighting-disinformation/search.html
Crash Course Navigating Digital Information:
   Go to YouTube and copy/paste the above description into the search bar for a lively 10-part series
   covering all aspects of navigating the digital world.
Campus Library, UW Bothell and Cascadia College
   https://guides.lib.uw.edu/c.php?g=345925&p=7772376
UW Center for an Informed Public:
   https://www.cip.uw.edu/
Arizona State University media literacy course:
   https://mediactive.newscollab.org

Back to Table of Contents
Back to study

Pink slime sites in Washington

Among Metric Media LLC's publications in Washington state as of September 2022 are the listed below 22 sites. Media watchers identify the publications as "pink slime."[126]

The fact-checker website Media Bias/Fact Check rates Metric Media as a "questionable source," saying "Overall, we rate Metric Media LLC right-center biased and questionable based on a lack of transparency, the publication of false information, and nondisclosure of over 1,000 imposter websites that are designed to look like local news sources."

Metric Media's pink slime websites likely are not the only such publications in Washington. Legitimate news publications make it easy to find the names of owners within their publications and on their websites.

East King News

Evergreen Reporter

Kitsap Review

Moses Lake Today

NE Washington News

NW Washington News

North King News

North Snohomish News

Olympic Times

Pierce Today

SE Washington News

Seattle City Wire

South King News

South Snohomish News

South Sound Times

Spokane County Times

Spokane Standard

Tri Cities Reporter

Vancouver Reporter

Washington Isle News

Wenatchee Times

Yakima Times

The News Literacy Project has produced a poster explaining how to vet a news source:

https://newslit.org/wp-content/uploads/2021/11/IsItLegit_infographic.pdf

Back to Table of Contents
Back to study

Publications for WA ethnic communities

Other papers serving the Black community

- Newspapers discussed in the main section of this report include **The Seattle Medium**, **The Black Lens**, and the **South Seattle Emerald**.
- **The Facts,** a weekly paper that has a circulation of more than 80,000, serves the Black community around Puget Sound. It has a digital presence as well as a print edition and describes itself as the "voice of the Black community."
- **The Skanner** has its primary office in Portland and a second office in Seattle. Established in 1975, it ceased its regular print publication in 2020, but continues with a digital publication.

Other Spanish-Language newspapers

- **El Sol de Yakima** is discussed in the main section of this report.
- **La Raza del Noroeste,** is associated with Sound Publishing's The Daily Herald in Everett.
- **La Voz,** is published in Pasco and distributed in Tri-Cities and in several communities throughout central and south central Washington.
- **El Periodico**, a Spanish-language section of the Lynden Tribune, is published in Whatcom County by Lewis Publishing.

Tribal nation publications

- A number of tribal nations recognized by the federal government produce news publications in Washington state. Click here for more details.

Newspapers serving Asian communities

- The bilingual **North American Post,** founded in 1902 by immigrants from Japan, is published twice a month.
- **Soy Source**, is a Japanese-language newspaper published by North American Post twice a month.
- **The Seattle Chinese Post,** founded in 1927 is the oldest Chinese-language newspaper in the Pacific Northwest.
- **Northwest Asian Weekly,** is a free English-language weekly published by the Seattle Chinese Post.
- **Seattle Chinese Times,** is a free bilingual weekly founded in 2004.
- **Northwest Vietnamese News,** a weekly, was founded by Vietnamese refugees in 1986.

Ethnic media outlets serving the Seattle area

https://www.seattle.gov/iandraffairs/EMP
Scroll to the bottom of the website for an exhaustive list of ethnic media outlets serving the Seattle area.

Back to Table of Contents
Back to study

Washington voting data 2008 to 2021

Percentage of Registered Voters Casting a Special Election Ballot

	Mar. 11, 2008	Feb. 3, 2009	Feb. 9, 2010	Feb. 8, 2011	Feb. 14, 2012	Feb. 12, 2013	Feb. 11, 2014	Feb. 10, 2015	Feb. 9, 2016	Feb. 14, 2017	Feb. 13, 2018	Feb. 12, 2019	Feb. 11, 2020	Feb. 9, 2021
					https://www.sos.wa.gov/elections/research/election-results-and-voters-pamphlets.aspx									
Adams	32.22		45.39	37.63	42.24	94.29	38.06	25.00	54.44	36.74	37.55	18.12	35.66	40.00
Asotin			51.26	59.11	51.31		46.71		44.74		35.80	46.84	37.86	
Benton		41.01	43.57	62.00	41.31	42.78	35.85	38.76	35.25	36.08	31.97	33.99	29.78	
Chehalis		45.56	49.30	54.98	47.99	49.53	43.10	52.73	46.06	44.19	40.17	44.40	45.05	41.41
Clallum			58.12	49.67	52.55	50.49		52.57	61.29	47.19	43.74		50.45	47.27
Clark	43.63		44.19		39.36	37.49	30.48	40.51	32.05	35.84	31.24	32.29	34.11	39.06
Columbia			65.18	54.85	56.91		64.29	49.33	57.77		49.92		51.95	
Cowlitz	44.02	47.03	44.02	44.88	44.42		34.08	39.04		36.06	35.37		40.70	39.09
Douglas		48.63	50.65	54.70	55.72	37.40	47.24	2.88	5.01	48.28	46.49	50.43	44.15	39.60
Ferry					56.66	47.45		53.72	58.25		47.49	51.96	49.23	
Franklin		57.22	43.80		44.71	44.06	33.98		33.66	30.85	29.91	17.28	34.92	
Garfield			63.73	56.75	71.95	55.28		55.65		53.75		47.64		
Grant	70.00	46.07	49.06	51.39	44.57	58.10	41.46	45.23	43.41	47.25	34.83	39.25	36.04	37.12
Grays Harbor	53.26	44.66	46.94	51.19	42.56	35.48	36.32	34.62	36.50	35.10	31.39	27.28	36.46	31.33
Island		42.16	54.84		55.00	48.51	41.46		43.63	42.26	44.00	45.17	43.52	40.18
Jefferson	55.37		61.87	58.27	56.15	47.65	49.79	54.14	55.25	50.25	51.07	43.68	48.73	47.26
King			40.01	60.00	33.91		30.99	35.75	28.16	39.09	31.83	30.73	32.71	
Kitsap	no data	no data	no data	no data	no data	no data	38.91	52.20	39.42	44.09	33.45	33.71	28.37	39.89
Kittitas	no data	no data	no data	no data	46.00	48.30	38.00	49.44	39.04	25.64	35.22	35.68	43.24	43.90
Klickitat		71.09	52.15	61.15	48.65	50.82	43.64	47.71	49.94	41.37	42.89	45.91	45.05	47.26
Lewis		51.44	47.68	49.05	45.44	46.72	38.77	41.41	39.69	42.36	36.62	42.52	39.18	34.73
Lincoln	54.99	57.99	56.36	55.07	60.90	52.39	49.29	50.89	53.68	48.33	47.06	49.57	48.39	48.14
Mason			52.02	44.85	51.08	48.67	36.48	46.68	42.43	38.95	39.72	39.34	39.96	39.71
Okanogan		55.04	50.11	42.63	48.86	50.75	43.28	45.25	47.80	42.42	41.01	37.90	43.09	
Pacific	51.76		54.98	57.43	52.24	66.08	53.76	51.86	43.33	45.20	44.70	42.62	45.98	38.52
Pend Oreille	52.59	39.68		53.71			47.69	39.74		44.86	40.34		47.39	35.64
Pierce			37.98	36.44	38.89	35.92	29.47	26.73	31.58	41.01	27.76	41.45	34.21	
San Juan			58.37	62.95	64.57	52.90	50.08		50.46	51.98			48.97	
Skagit			51.05	46.01	45.32	47.83	41.11	61.08	38.79	34.61	40.75	36.73	45.06	35.75
Skamania			45.62		57.57		38.01	41.54		33.54			41.29	42.90
Snohomish		23.04	36.51		34.02	33.42	28.42	30.18	29.78	32.59	30.80	22.44	33.02	26.62
Spokane	37.64	47.43	43.65	50.63	48.48	35.68	43.28	40.16	36.06	34.88	36.62	31.69	35.52	39.77
Stevens	57.13	55.19	50.50		56.76	52.97	47.40	50.05	49.24	35.17	42.53	38.84	45.57	41.76
Thurston			43.12		38.91		34.09	32.05	34.88	27.84	33.98	35.26	35.92	
Wahkiakum			56.28		55.90	61.80	42.93	46.99			45.41		62.66	44.46
Walla Walla			52.55	51.99	50.44	52.77	40.15	48.77	44.16	48.79	37.20	37.93	41.68	
Whatcom			47.04	50.01	43.07	47.06	43.69	33.94	36.15		32.58	43.63	37.55	21.62
Whitman	52.50	54.87	53.40	54.22	46.34	41.59	40.54	46.94	38.06	45.55	36.33	36.11	35.93	41.16
Yakima		52.17	44.05	51.76	52.05	35.36	34.42	30.60	30.02	37.65	32.30	37.08	31.99	33.42
% voting by year	**50.43**	**48.90**	**49.87**	**52.26**	**49.27**	**48.69**	**41.03**	**42.69**	**41.47**	**40.58**	**38.33**	**38.05**	**41.09**	**39.17**

We tested whether voter turnout declined in any of Washington's 39 counties over the years 2004 through 2021 when newspapers were experiencing declining content, consolidation, staffing losses and reductions in print circulation.

We chose the special elections that occur in early spring and involve nonpartisan county- or city-level bond and funding issues for police, libraries, schools and fire departments.

The few single digit turnout numbers in the chart indicate a fire or school district that crosses county lines.

Figure 22 Credit: News study committee

Back to Table of Contents
Back to study

Understanding algorithms

What are social media algorithms?

An algorithm is a set of rules computer coders write to sort and rank search results and other data.

For example, Facebook algorithms direct that posts from friends will appear on feeds before those of strangers. Those who frequently click on pictures of cute puppies on Instagram will see more pictures of cute puppies on that platform because an algorithm "learns" this preference.

The idea is to mimic human decision making to display content that social media users are likely to want to see. The algorithm then can make recommendations for pages to like, videos to watch, or ads likely to elicit a response — dog food, for example.

The down side to this interaction is privacy. Algorithms use personal data to "learn" how to display content relevant to a user: geographic location, social media friends, pages and hashtags searched for, and what a user is clicking on, reading, and watching. Algorithms can influence how social-media users think and feel, and this has been a source of controversy for all social media platforms.[127]

For example, in 2017, Facebook assigned point values to emoji reactions: "love," "haha," "wow," "sad," and "angry," giving maximum points to "angry." It is well researched that negative social media posts get far more attention than positive posts, so the change drove algorithms to disproportionately feature controversial posts, according to The Washington Post.[128]

Facebook officials knew it was possible that favoring controversial posts was likely to lead to more spam and online abuse.

The result?

"The company's data scientists confirmed in 2019 that posts sparking angry reaction emoji were disproportionately likely to include misinformation, toxicity and low-quality news," the Post reported.

Back to Table of Contents
Back to study

Malheur Enterprise digs into finance

Malheur County sprawls over nearly 10,000 square miles in southeast Oregon: rural, sparsely populated, and the poorest of the state's 36 counties.

The **Malheur Enterprise** covers events familiar to rural residents, like the Easter egg hunt, the book club meeting, and the county commissioners' meeting – typical fare of a weekly paper with a circulation of 3,000. But the bonus in this tiny, one-newspaper town is the investigative reporting the Enterprise provides, which can stand alongside the journalistic investigation by any big-city daily.

The Enterprise's efforts illustrate the significant role a newspaper – even a small newspaper – can play when it reports important developments, including information some in power don't want others to know about.

The Enterprise attracted national attention three years ago when it published a series of stories about the multiple public jobs held simultaneously by its contract economic development director, Greg Smith. Smith, also an elected member of the Oregon House of Representatives, raked in more than $830,000 from those jobs in 2018 alone.[129]

Malheur County paid him more than $100,000 that year. Other agencies he worked for in 2018 included Wheeler County, Eastern Oregon University, Baker County, and Harney County. Smith also had contracts paid with public funds from Morrow Development Corp., Umatilla Electric Cooperative in Hermiston, and Linn Economic Development Group in Albany.

The stories raised questions about how Smith, as a state representative, can separate his private interests from his public duties. "As a legislator, Smith can influence every state agency budget in his role as a vice chair of the Legislature's budget-writing committee," the Enterprise reported. "His public and private hats come off and on at his will." [130]

Shortly after the story ran, county officials asked the Malheur County sheriff to open a criminal investigation into the Enterprise for harassment, specifically for making too many phone calls and sending too many emails to Smith and his employees during the reporting process. The sheriff declined to investigate. [131]

The dogged reporting by the Malheur Enterprise, in Vale, Oregon, illustrates the ability of a newspaper, even a small-town paper, to publish stories that some in power don't want public. Credit: Google Maps, image capture: Oct. 2018, © 2022 Google

The Enterprise's June 2019 reporting won first place in politics and government reporting and was runner-up for investigative reporting in a Society of Professional Journalists regional newspaper competition.[132]
Although Smith lost some of his public economic development jobs in the aftermath, despite the publicity about the apparent conflicts, the Oregon Government Ethics Commission did not take any action against him.[133]

More recently, the Enterprise drilled down on Smith's body of work for Malheur County over nine years, under the headline "Economic Development: Malheur County officials struggle to tell what $900,000 bought." Reporters spent six months poring over county records and interviewing county and economic development officials to produce what it called "the first independent accounting of the agency's performance."[134]

The results "show an agency without oversight, producing uncertain results, managed by remote control from Heppner." Smith lives in Heppner.

> "Malheur County officials struggle to tell what $900,000 bought"
> — Enterprise headline

The reporters said Smith could produce no work plan and no annual report, and that the three county commissioners who sign his contract every year had to be given talking points by Smith to explain how he had attracted jobs and businesses to Malheur.

Despite the investigative reporting, Smith continues to serve in the Oregon House of Representatives. He was sworn in to his 11th consecutive term in 2021.

The publisher of the Enterprise, Les Zaitz, is a longtime reporter and was a Pulitzer Prize finalist twice. He bought the newspaper in 2015, and had been hoping to sell it and retire soon. A week after publication of the "$900,000" story, Zaitz received a buyout offer from Smith. In a letter to Zaitz, Smith offered $35,000 to buy the business, "no employees included." Smith claimed "locals are begging for you to sell this community newspaper."[135]

In response, Zaitz posted on the Enterprise's Facebook page about Smith's buyout offer and asked, "Would you like new owners for this 113-year-old paper? Should Greg Smith's offer be taken seriously?" Zaitz published many of the 800 comments he received asking him not to sell the Enterprise, especially not to Greg Smith.

In an interview published by Nieman Lab in March 2022, Zaitz said, "The Enterprise is going to go to someone who has experience in journalism, who wants to take this newspaper to the next level and ensure this doesn't become a news desert."

In an update in late 2022, Zaitz said Smith "opted not to renew his contract for economic development services because of the 'toxic' environment," but continues to manage the rail shipping center for Malheur County. County commissioners increased his pay from $6,000 per month to $9,000.

The Enterprise is suing the county to obtain public records, and the county district attorney has recently ordered disclosure of some records, Zaitz said.

Back to Table of Contents
Back to study

Will philanthropy save the day?

The Columbian innovation editor Will Campbell said he and his brother, Ben, the publisher, are intent on ensuring their family-owned newspaper will continue to serve future generations of southwest Washington readers. That commitment, he said, is one of the reasons the Campbells partnered with the Local Media Association, a nonprofit organization best described as a fiscal sponsor.

Campbell said the association, along with its affiliate, the Local Media Foundation, are all about promoting the sustainability of local journalism. At The Columbian, that means providing fundraising guidance as well as a system approved by the Internal Revenue Service for accepting tax-deductible donations.

The association is one of a handful of nonprofit fiscal sponsors created in recent years to help local news outlets deal with today's economic challenges. Others include Journalism Funding Partners, which began as the McClatchy Journalism Institute; Report for America; and Innovia, with which The Spokesman-Review in Spokane has partnered.

Newspapers in some communities also have affiliated with local foundations that enable them to collect tax-deductible donations, including the Seattle Foundation, the Yakima Valley Community Foundation, and the Community Foundation of Snohomish County. Other Washington state papers with fiscal sponsors include The Daily Herald in Everett, The Bellingham Herald, The Olympian, the Yakima Herald-Republic, and The Seattle Times.

It was The Seattle Times' success partnering with the Local Media Association and the Seattle Foundation, in fact, that convinced leadership at The Columbian to pursue a fiscal sponsor. "The Seattle Times was a pioneer in this," Campbell said. "They've been at this for 10 years."

At the Times, publisher Frank Blethen had been working for the last couple of decades lobbying against media consolidation. In 2019 he established the Free Press Initiative, a multimedia attempt to educate the public, academics, and lawmakers about the history and importance of newspapers, and to establish a national dialogue about the importance of local media.

His outreach to the U.S. senators and representatives serving Washington is most likely responsible for the near-unanimous agreement among the legislators that there should be some kind of legislation supporting local news.

Local Media Association officials provide advice on crowdfunding and all aspects of fundraising – from language to use in an email to a prospective donor to how to develop a marketing plan.

"They've given us best practices," Campbell said. "Without the Local Media Foundation's help, we would be lost in trying to raise money for local journalism." As of mid-April 2022, the association had enabled The Columbian to collect $1 million in pledges toward a $1.6 million goal, enough to add four journalists for up to six years, Campbell said.

The reporters will cover transportation, housing, and homelessness, significant concerns in southwest Washington.

Campbell said IRS laws are highly specific and association guidance helps ensure donations meet the strict regulations, which include making sure the funds go only to appropriate expenses: the salaries, training, and travel of the financed reporters.

Other papers that partner with the Local Media Association also hire reporters to "focus on enterprise or investigative reporting on critical community issues such as social justice, poverty, the unhoused, education, or health inequities," according to the nonprofit's website.

Report for America

Launched in 2017, Report for America provides seed money to qualifying newspapers to report on under-covered issues and communities. Journalists are assigned for a year with an option to serve two years, which most do.[136]

The first year, Report for America pays half of a journalist's salary. The local news organization pays the other half, ideally from local donations or in collaboration with local nonprofits.

Report for America holds two competitions, one for media outlets to make their case that they have "urgent gaps in coverage," and another for "talented emerging journalists … to serve these communities."

In Washington, since the first Report for America reporter was assigned in 2019 to The Spokesman-Review, the service program has placed 13 reporters with six media outlets:

- The Daily Herald, Everett.
- The News Tribune, Tacoma.
- The News Tribune in partnership with The Olympian, The Bellingham Herald, and the Tri-City Herald.
- The Olympian.
- The Spokesman-Review, Spokane .
- The Yakima Herald-Republic.

As of February 2022, nine Report for America reporters had been financed for Washington newsrooms to cover underserved communities and issues for 2022-23:

- Two in Everett, with one focused on working-class issues and the other on education.
- One at The News Tribune in partnership with The Olympian, The Bellingham Herald, and the Tri-City Herald to cover Indigenous communities in the state. Natasha Brennan is in her second year with Report for America on this assignment.
- One reporter, Brandon Block, to cover homelessness issues until May 2022 at The Olympian.
- Three reporters at The Spokesman-Review: Laurel Demkovich in her second year as a statehouse reporter; Orion Donovan-Smith in his second year at the capitol in Washington, D.C., covering legislation affecting the Northwest; and a reporter to be selected to focus on rural areas in eastern Washington.
- Two at the Yakima Herald-Republic, one covering economic and educational issues in the Latino community and one writing about rural health care in Yakima County.

The Spokesman-Review executive editor Rob Curley said the newspaper's relationship with Report for America has been essential for the paper in being able to report on topics that most regional daily newsrooms no longer have the resources to cover. "Report for America has been a game changer for us," Curley said in a 2021 article in The Spokesman-Review.[137]

The paper has expanded coverage, emphasizing the importance of serving rural Washington and Idaho, Curley said. The partnership that Report for America has enabled the paper to develop with the community has paid off in other ways.

"We've also been able to show our community what it is like for a news organization to work closely with its readers to not only identify topics they'd like to see us write more about, but also to work directly with us to get those sorts of new reporter positions funded," he said.

As a result, The Spokesman-Review has "one of the most unique newsrooms in the nation. And none of it happens without the help we have received from Report for America," Curley said.

Stories by reporters financed with Report for America and other community dollars feature a Creative Commons license, meaning other organizations also may publish the work.

Journalism Funding Partners

Journalism Funding Partners began as the McClatchy Journalism Institute to promote relationships between financiers and McClatchy-owned news organizations. In time, the board expanded the organization's reach, opening its doors to papers with other owners. Journalism Funding Partners is an IRS-certified nonprofit.[138]

The volunteer board members are professional journalists, most of whom were McClatchy newspaper employees prior to Chatham Asset Management's 2020 purchase of the chain.

As with the Report for America and Local Media Association programs, Journalism Funding Partners reporters are hired with a particular focus area in mind, according to its website.

At The Daily Herald in Everett, it is the fiscal sponsor for the Investigative Journalism Fund supporting investigative reporting in Everett and Snohomish County communities, and the Environmental and Climate Change Reporting Fund — created to "shed light on the local impacts brought about by climate change."[139]

Besides a means for collecting tax-deductible contributions, Journalism Funding Partners also provides fundraising guidance and promotes journalism philanthropy in the community. The nonprofit describes the three-pronged effort as a new business model for newspapers today.

Back to Table of Contents
Back to study

What is nonprofit news?

Journalism nonprofits have been in existence for more than 175 years. In 1846, five New York newspapers banded together to share reporting from the Mexican-American War, giving birth to The Associated Press. Today, the AP is a global nonprofit cooperative owned by member newspapers in the United States.

More than 400 news organizations are members of the Institute for Nonprofit News. They include national investigative reporting operations, publications specializing in particular topics such as equity or climate, and local newsrooms filling the role traditionally held by for-profit newspapers.

The news operations are typically 501(c)(3) organizations under the federal tax code. That designation makes them tax-exempt charities that are restricted from paying out profits to shareholders or investors. They must be nonpartisan and dedicated to public service.

Nonprofit news organizations are not allowed to endorse candidates for office and are restricted in political activity.

More state nonprofit news outlets

Key Peninsula News in Vaughn was founded in 1976 as a newsletter for the Key Peninsula Civic Center Association, but it has been financially and editorially independent since 1989.

"It being completely independent is very helpful to journalism, to not have to answer to another entity that is not journalism oriented, where they want to get involved in your choices of what you've covered or how you covered it," executive editor Lisa Bryan said. "And there was definitely some pressure to do that on editors, like, 'Gosh, you know, we could really use a story promoting our fundraiser,' or that kind of thing."

Local businesses' ad sales, along with donations from individuals and organizations, support the monthly print newspaper. The Institute for Nonprofit News' NewsMatch program also has contributed. Bryan said local advertisers prefer the lower rates and local audience the News offers compared with those of larger newspapers such as The News Tribune.

"We've received over $50,000 in contributions and from people that send in a check for $5, all the way to people that are writing checks for $2,500," Bryan said. "There's been a buy-in; the community feels like, 'This is our paper.'"

The News is mailed monthly to every household in the county for free. There are no plans to print more frequently, but the newspaper's website is updated with breaking news if warranted before the monthly paper is published. The website draws about 14,000 monthly unique viewers in a county of 19,000 residents, Bryan said.

"We really strongly believe that every citizen deserves news that's relevant to their community, that's fair and accurate and nonpartisan. That is a big deal to us to put a print edition in every mailbox, whether you asked for it or not," Bryan said. "We want our voters to be educated, no matter what."

Without the News, people would rely on social media for information and "there's so much disinformation out there," she said. "A lot of people aren't reading any local news at all. They're just reading national news and being wrapped up in that. And that's not healthy for democracy."

Bryan said she believes nonprofit journalism is the best approach. "It does restrict you from endorsing candidates, but there are bigger newspapers that do that kind of thing," she said.

Instead, the News sponsors candidate forums that draw large crowds during election season. "It's huge, people are interested, they want to meet their candidates, they want to ask questions and so we sponsor that," Bryan said.

"People do trust us from all across the political spectrum. There's a level of trust that we have developed. … And I believe that model can be replicated everywhere," she added.

The JOLT – The Journal of Olympia, Lacey and Tumwater – was founded in 2020 by Danny Stusser, who formerly owned the local franchise of the Coffee News, advertising printed on placemats and distributed at restaurants.

The online JOLT has four paid part-time reporters and five freelance columnists. The reporters cover area city and county commissions and school boards. "It's been 25 years since the newspaper tried to cover all the public meetings here," executive director Stusser said. It is a sizable task, Stusser said, given that Thurston County has 100 government councils, boards and commissions that should be covered. Sections include business, local politics, education, environment, the Legislature, real estate, breaking news, editorials, letters to the editor, community calendar, police blotter, food, travel, outdoors and obituaries.

The publication drew initial financing from the Nisqually Indian Tribe, a dozen local businesses, and about 45 individuals who contributed between $9 and $500 each, Stusser said. In September 2021, Stusser converted to nonprofit status so The JOLT would qualify for the INN's NewsMatch program.

"NewsMatch is fabulous," he said. "I'm looking forward to getting the significant amount of paperwork done so that we qualify for the maximum $14,000 of match funds."

Stusser has been surprised by how many candidates for elected positions run unopposed. "It's not necessarily because everybody agreed that the incumbents were doing a great job," he said. "I think one of the things that we can do is bring issues to people's minds. And by paying attention, maybe they become more interested in running for office."

Salish Current, in Bellingham, serves Whatcom, San Juan and Skagit counties. It produces a weekly online wrap-up of local news about government, law enforcement, public health, education, agriculture, and business, and diversity, equity, and inclusion.

Current reporters do not staff local council meetings. Instead, the publication posts the agendas and video links to the meetings. The publication is financed by donations from foundations and individuals, community events, sponsorships, and subscribers, according to its website.

A recent free event, held in conjunction with a local bookstore, was "Trust 2022: Why Independent Local News is Important to a Strong Democracy," featuring state Attorney General Bob Ferguson and journalists Margaret Sullivan, formerly of The Washington Post, and Hedrick Smith, formerly of The New York Times.

InvestigateWest was founded by former Seattle Post-Intelligencer reporters after the paper stopped publishing its print edition in 2009. While it also covers British Columbia and Oregon, the website emphasizes Washington state issues.

Focusing on environment, government, corporate accountability, and public health, InvestigateWest has won more than 75 awards since 2010. "We produce original reporting and tools that equip the public to participate in our democracy," InvestigateWest's mission statement says.

InvestigateWest's website says its work has resulted in new state laws to protect workers, the environment, and foster children. One story explored voter signature rejections in Washington, finding that in eight counties, ballots from Latino voters were twice as likely to be rejected.

One area the organization won't cover is the horse race aspect of elections, said executive director Jacob Fries. "I don't imagine necessarily doing singular race stories, but I could see doing trends," he said. For example, "here's three races that could shift the power balance in Olympia."

Financing comes from foundations, major donors, and some individuals, Fries said. The organization has one full-time reporter plus a "feisty band of freelancers" across Washington, he said. Also on staff are three part-time senior editors and some interns.

InvestigateWest is involved in the INN's Rural News Network, a consortium of nonprofit news organizations reporting on rural America, as well as Washington State University's Rural Reporting Project, which connects student journalists with rural communities.

Fries' advice to someone thinking of starting a nonprofit news operation is to ask oneself:

- What are you doing?
- Have you studied the market?
- How are you differentiating yourself from others?
- What value will you add to the community?
- Why would anyone want to either give you a donation or advertise?

"So I think doing an analysis of what they're trying to accomplish, and how they're going to fit into the ecosystem of information that already exists. And then I'd probably tell them, you hopefully have already done this work for somebody else before you've become self employed."

Crosscut is part of Cascade Public Media, which also owns public television station KCTS. The multimedia website says it "strives to provide readers with the facts and analysis they need to intelligently participate in civic discourse, and to create a more just, equitable and sustainable society."

In early 2022, Crosscut had 28 employees, with reporters in Yakima, Spokane, Olympia, and the Puget Sound area. Its text stories are republished in newspapers and websites throughout the state. Crosscut also is looking at ways to share its broadcast content with those audiences.

Unlike traditional daily newspapers, Crosscut does not cover "every turn of the screw" with daily spot stories on legislative meetings, instead focusing on broader enterprise pieces, said managing editor Mark Baumgarten.

Videos include interviews with newsmakers, a series on environmental justice, and more. Podcast topics include current events, outdoor adventures, and youth.

Statewide projects have included a series on police accountability, a story about how a local helmet law was being enforced mostly on the homeless population, and continuing coverage around equity in the health care industry.

Crosscut works with longtime Washington state pollster Stuart Elway, who conducts quarterly polling with annual surveys focusing on elections and legislative priorities. M. David Lee III, the executive editor, said Crosscut also hires a freelancer to track select bills through the Legislature.

Crosscut publishes a voter guide that asks questions posed by readers to candidates. Election coverage centers on issues. And it's part of the state debate coalition, helping sponsor debates on the local and state level. Last year, Crosscut hosted two Seattle mayoral debates.

The Crosscut Festival, "a celebration of big ideas and bold thinking," is an annual event featuring more than 50 speakers and draws more than 2,000 attendees. Other events include monthly gatherings of Northwest newsmakers. There is no charge for attending these events.

Much of Crosscut's financing comes from its association with PBS. "'Antiques Roadshow' puts bread on my table," Baumgarten said. Grants, advertising and memberships – at $5 a month – also bring in funds. He said PBS provides "a large percentage of our operating budget," but he declined to share specific numbers.

A grant from Group Health Foundation, for example, is financing investigative work around how federal dollars are spent in rural communities in the state – something that smaller news organizations can't afford to do.

Like the other nonprofits, Crosscut does not charge for access to its website. "We thought that was very important. What we're doing is serving the community, and as a public nonprofit newsroom, we want to make sure that everybody has the opportunity to get what we're sharing," Baumgarten said.

Baumgarten praised the INN's efforts to improve reporting in rural areas. For example, Crosscut participates in a program that provides toolkits for reporting about census data for rural counties. And Crosscut's central Washington reporter participates in the INN's Rural News Network.

Two other Washington state nonprofits focus on social issues:

Seattle-based **Grist** was founded in 1999 to write about the environment, social justice, poverty, and hunger.

On Bainbridge Island, **YES! Media** is an online and print magazine that describes itself as "solutions journalism," analyzing social problems and exploring opportunities for change.

Can nonprofits remain solvent?

While those managing Washington's nonprofits are mostly upbeat about the future, remaining solvent continues to be a challenge.

The JOLT's Stusser said he had predictable revenue for only six months: "We go and sell a couple of ads or sponsorship agreements. We recruit a reporter or a columnist and we just keep the cycle going, and we keep it going until we're either exhausted or we get lucky."

That's dangerous territory, said Richard Tofel, the former president of ProPublica, the national nonprofit investigative news website. "In my view, it's a mistake to begin operations without at least 18 months of spending on hand, and two years is even better."

At the Key Peninsula News, many staffers work for free and others earn less than a living wage. "Everyone on our board of directors is aware of this problem," editor Bryan said. In 2022, she said, staff compensation increased 20% and the goal is to pay all key staffers and provide benefits.

Another challenge for nonprofits is that newsroom leaders also must double as nonprofit administrators, and writing grants is a new skill set for many.

But Sue Cross, the INN's CEO and executive director, noted that her organization provides support and training for new nonprofit news managers. She believes the continued growth of the nonprofit news industry shows that "sustainable business models exist for journalism rooted in civic purpose rather than profit."

She predicted that within 10 years, "independent, nonprofit newsrooms will produce a significant share of the news consumed by most Americans about our civic life."

Back to Table of Contents
Back to study

East Washingtonian: No government aid

In the southeastern Washington towns of Pomeroy and Dayton, populations 1,389 and 2,448, Charlotte Baker and her husband, Loyal, publish the East Washingtonian and Dayton Chronicle.[140]

They've owned the Chronicle since 2014, and the East Washingtonian since 2018, having purchased the papers with an eye on giving themselves meaningful jobs that also would allow them to retire with a little nest egg.

But they've been hit by the economic difficulties that have buffeted newspapers across the country. Circulation remains fairly steady at 800 at each paper, but advertising revenue has declined.

Clients who once bought print advertising in the papers are turning to Facebook, where they can advertise for free, reducing a key revenue source, Baker told the news study committee.

As internet access in rural areas improves, the situation only grows worse. "For bigger cities, Facebook is a has-been site," Baker said. "But in our community, we are behind and so once people get the internet, Facebook is a newfangled thing."

The Bakers are tightening their belts. Sometimes they don't pay themselves so they can pay the part-time reporter at each paper and their grandson, who earns minimum wage for handling subscriptions. They share stories and photos with other small weeklies. Baker is candid about her concerns. She said she and her husband never have seen times as tough economically as they are today. "We are absolutely worried about the future," she said.

The couple is familiar with legislation such as the Local Journalism Sustainability Act, which would provide tax credits to newspapers to offset salaries, to small businesses to buy newspaper advertisements and readers to buy subscriptions. But Baker said she and her husband can't support the bill.

"Of course, we all want money," Baker said. "But we are watchdogs of the government and we will never, ever accept money from the government or corporations." To do so would compromise the integrity of newspapering, she said.

In addition to producing the newspapers, Baker owns and operates a 40-year-old music studio where she teaches piano and voice. If economic conditions require it, she could increase her teaching to supplement their income.

Loyal, left, and Charlotte Baker publish the East Washingtonian and Dayton Chronicle in rural Washington.

But they won't quit publishing. "The papers ... give history to what is going on," Baker said. "As long as we are breathing, we are going to hold on."

Back to Table of Contents
Back to study

Proposed legislation

Figure 23

Federal	What it would do:	Current status:
House Bill 6068 Saving Local News Act 2021-2022 *Six co-sponsors, none from Washington https://www.congress.gov/bill/117th-congress/house-bill/6068/text.	This bill would amend the Internal Revenue Code of 1986 to include publication of written news articles as a tax-exempt purpose for organizations, and for other purposes.	Introduced in the House on Nov. 23, 2021 and referred to the House Ways and Means Committee.
Senate Bill 673 Journalism Competition and Preservation Act of 2021 2021-2022 *Seven co-sponsors (bipartisan) No sponsors from Washington https://www.congress.gov/bill/117th-congress/senate-bill/673.	This bill creates a four-year safe harbor from antitrust laws for *print, broadcast, or digital news companies to collectively* negotiate with online content distributors (e.g., social media companies) regarding the terms on which the news companies' content may be distributed by online content distributors.	Discussed at the Senate Judiciary *Subcommittee on Competition* Policy, antitrust, and Consumer Rights Feb. 2, 2022.
House Bill 1735 Journalism Competition and Preservation Act of 2021 *63 co-sponsors (bipartisan), including Rep. Jayapal from Washington https://www.congress.gov/bill/117th-congress/house-bill/1735?s=1&r=2.	This bill creates a four-year safe harbor from antitrust laws for print, broadcast, or digital news companies to collectively negotiate with online content distributors (e.g., social media companies) regarding terms under which the news companies' content may be distributed by online content distributors.	Referred to the Subcommittee on Antitrust, Commercial, and Administrative Law. Action by: Committee on the Judiciary May 18, 2021.
House Bill 3940 Local Journalism Sustainability Act 2021-2022 *72 co-sponsors (bipartisan) Introduced by Rep. Newhouse (R-WA) From Washington state Reps. Larson, DelBene, Herrera Beutler, Jayapal, Kilmer, Adam Smith, Strickland, and Schrier https://www.congress.gov/bill/117th-congress/house-bill/3940/.	This bill allows individual taxpayers a tax credit up to $250 in any taxable year for subscriptions to one or more local newspapers. It also allows a local news employer a payroll credit for wages paid to local news journalists. The bill allows certain small businesses a tax credit for advertising in a local newspaper or through a broadcast of a radio or television station serving a local community.	Referred to the House Ways and Means committee Jun. 16, 2021 [Part of the Build Back Better bill].
Senate Bill 2434 Local Journalism Sustainability Act 2021-2022 *17 co-sponsors Introduced by Sen. Cantwell (D-WA) from Washington state: Sen. Murray https://www.congress.gov/bill/117th-congress/senate-bill/2434.	This bill allows individual taxpayers a tax credit up to $250 in any taxable year for subscriptions to one or more local newspapers. It also allows a local news employer a payroll credit for wages paid to local news journalists. The bill allows certain small businesses a tax credit for advertising in a local newspaper or through a broadcast of a radio or television station serving a local community.	Referred to the Committee on Finance Jul. 22, 2021.
House Bill 3169 Future of Local News Act 2021-2022 *Five co-sponsors (bipartisan) No co-sponsors from Washington state https://www.congress.gov/bill/117th-congress/house-bill/3169.	This bill establishes the Future of Local News Committee to examine, report on, and make recommendations related to the state of local news and the ability of local news to meet the information needs of the people of the United States.	Sent to House Energy and Commerce Subcommittee on Communications and Technology and House Small Business Committee May 12, 2021.
Senate Bill 1601 Future of Local News Act 2021-2022 *Two co-sponsors No co-sponsors from Washington state https://www.congress.gov/bill/117th-congress/senate-bill/1601.	This bill establishes the Future of Local News Committee to examine, report on, and make recommendations related to the state of local news and the ability of local news to meet the information needs of the people of the United States.	Read twice and referred to the Committee on Commerce, Science, and Transportation.
Senate Bill 2457 PRESS Act Protect Reporters from Excessive State Suppression Act *One sponsor – Sen. Wyden (D-OR) https://www.congress.gov/bill/117th-congress/senate-bill/2457/text.	A bill to maintain the free flow of information to the public by establishing appropriate limits on the federally compelled disclosure of information obtained as part of engaging in journalism, and for other purposes.	Referred to the Committee on the Judiciary Jul. 22, 2021.
House Resolution 821 Expressing the sense of the House of Representatives regarding the importance of local print and digital journalism to the continued welfare, transparency, and prosperity of government at every level and the continuation and freedom of the United States as it is known today. 2021-2022 *Three co-sponsors, no co-sponsors from Washington https://www.congress.gov/bill/117th-congress/house-resolution/821/text.	*Resolved,* That it is the sense of the House of Representatives that— *(1) It is in the best interests of federal, state, and local governments to make all possible efforts to ensure the continuation of robust local digital and print news sources; and* *(2) Congress should work with news outlets and other relevant stakeholders to ensure that local digital and print news continues to operate in a robust manner for years to come.*	Referred to the House Committee on Oversight and Reform Nov. 23, 2021.

Washington State	What it would do:	Current status:
Senate Bill 5541 2022 Sponsored by: Sens. Mullet, Gildon, Keiser, Lilas, and Lovick https://legiscan.com/WA/bill/SB5541/2021.	This bill would have exempted newspapers in Washington from paying the Business and Occupation tax.	Discussed in Senate Committee on Business, Financial Services & Trade Jan. 20, 2021 Failed to get out of committee.

Local Journalism Sustainability Act

The fate of the Local Journalism Sustainability Act is unclear.

Included in President Joe Biden's $3.5 trillion Build Back Better bill, the act's prospects dimmed when the president's plan was derailed, according to Rick Edmonds of the Poynter Institute.[141]

The act proposes a tax credit of up to $250 to subscribers of local newspapers; tax credits of up to half of the salary of a local news journalist up to $50,000; and tax credits of up to $5,000 to local businesses to advertise in newspapers. To qualify, a news outlet would have to primarily serve the needs of a regional or local community and could not employ more than 750 employees.

In spring 2022, the act had 17 Senate co-sponsors, all Democrats, including Washington's Patty Murray and Maria Cantwell. In the House, it had support from both sides, including nine of Washington's 10 representatives. Republican Rep. Cathy McMorris Rodgers, from eastern Washington, was not a supporter.

Two other Washington elected officials have publicized their support for the act: Attorney General Bob Ferguson and Treasurer Mike Pellicciotti. Both helped persuade their colleagues in other states, with Ferguson leading 15 other attorneys general to sign a letter of support.[142]

"Without good journalism and good oversight, you lose that public watchdog component that allows for good governance to take root and continue," Pellicciotti said.

Journalism Competition and Preservation Act

Another key piece of federal legislation is the Journalism Competition and Preservation Act. Sen. Amy Klobuchar, D-Minnesota, is the lead sponsor of the bill, also known as the Safe Harbor Act. The name signifies protection from antitrust laws for news outlets seeking to negotiate collectively with Google and Facebook for Big Tech's use of their content.

Perhaps surprising, Microsoft supports the act. All participants in the "news technology ecosystem ... have both an opportunity and responsibility to help journalism flourish. We recognize that we should start with ourselves," company president Brad Smith told a House subcommittee.[143]

The only Washington representative who had expressed support for the act by early 2022 was Democrat Pramila Jayapal, who represents the Seattle area. The Seattle Times publisher Frank Blethen and other supporters argue that it's reasonable for Google, Facebook, and others to compensate news outlets for the stories their reporters produce. After all, readers can access them, sometimes for free, on Big Tech sites. But opponents argue that the stories themselves don't produce Big Tech's revenues.

Rather, they say it's the advertising that Big Tech sells alongside the news reports. Opponents also argue that by featuring the news articles, the tech companies regularly drive traffic back to the news outlets' sites.[144] [145]

The Future of Local News Act

Bills in both the House and the Senate call for creating a federal Future of Local News Committee to examine, report on, and make recommendations on local news' ability to meet America's information needs. The advisory panel would study the impact of the loss of local newspapers, digital news outlets, and broadcasting outlets; assess COVID-19's effect on local news organizations; and propose solutions.[146]

Saving The Local News Act

This act would address Internal Revenue Service requirements to allow for-profit news organizations to convert to nonprofit or public purpose status, as the Salt Lake Tribune did when it reincorporated as a 501(c)(3).

Legislation proposed in Washington state

In January 2022, state Sen. Mark Mullet, D-Issaquah, introduced Senate Bill 5541. He did so not long after a Washington Joint Legislative Audit and Review Committee noted newspaper revenues in Washington had fallen an average of $27 million per year over the last five years. The bill would have reduced the business and occupation tax on newspapers to zero. Twelve years earlier, the Legislature reduced it to 0.35%, but that provision expires in July 2024.

Opening the hearing, Mullet was blunt: "People on the left and right tell me this idea stinks."

Sen. Lynda Wilson, R-Battle Ground, was among the opposition, suggesting it best to let the market determine the fate of newspapers. "But if we did this for every business that was failing, like manufacturing…" she said.

A few months earlier, The Seattle Times had pointed out such preferential tax rates aren't unique to publishers. Brier Dudley, the paper's Free Press editor, reported Washington provides dozens of B&O preferences to solar-energy system manufacturers, affordable housing developers, and dairy producers.

At the hearing, Rowland Thompson, executive director of Allied Daily Newspapers of Washington, said publishers and owners "feel a calling to produce news about their local communities. What they bring to the community is extremely important. They tend to stitch the social fabric of communities together even as thin as they are today."

By the end of the day, the bill didn't have the votes to make it out of committee, reported Mullet's senior legislator assistant, Adam Day.

Legislation proposed In other states

Other states have proposed and adopted legislation to support newspapers. Here are a few:

Wisconsin: The Wisconsin Local Media Advertising Tax Credit would provide tax credits to small businesses that advertise in newspapers, on TV or radio stations, or on online media. Credits would be available to advertisers with fewer than 100 employees and less than $10 million in revenue.[147]

Colorado: A bill similar to the Wisconsin tax credit has been introduced in the Legislature.[148]

New York, New Jersey, and Virginia: The three states have versions of advertising tax credit legislation. New Jersey already provides some financing for a local news innovation fund.[149]

New Jersey: Gov. Phil Murphy's 2021 budget included $500,000 to kickstart the New Jersey Civic Information Consortium, a 501(c)(3) nonprofit to improve "civic life information" needs.[150]

New York City: Mayors Bill de Blasio and Eric Adams have directed that at least half of government advertising be placed in local media.[151]

Illinois: Gov. J.B. Pritzker signed legislation in summer 2021 to create a 15-person Local Journalism Task Force to study communities underserved by local journalism. Recommendations are due Jan. 1, 2023.[152]

Massachusetts: In 2021, the state approved the creation of a commission to study journalism in underserved communities.[153]

Washington publishers, editors speak on legislation

In March 2021, the news study queried Washington newspaper owners and publishers about their positions on the Local Journalism Sustainability Act:

The Wenatchee World publisher **Sean Flaherty**: "We support it. In fact, our newspaper company's CEO, Francis Wick, worked with Reps. Newhouse and Kirkpatrick early on."

Senior Scene, serving Pierce and King counties, editor **Pat Jenkins**: "Yes, it's an intriguing proposal that isn't perfect but at least is a step. And I support any government or other public assistance that supports media without jeopardizing media's independence."

Lynden Tribune and Ferndale Record publisher/president **Michael D. Lewis**: "Yes, I absolutely support this bill. If something is not done soon to rein in Facebook and Google, community newspapers will be a thing of the past, which is a travesty." (Note: This bill doesn't address Big Tech; the Journalism Competition and Preservation Act does.)

The Columbian publisher **Ben Campbell:** "The Local Journalism Sustainability Act has been on my radar since it was created early last year and it's something that I think would be tremendously helpful to The Columbian and many other local media companies looking to sustain quality local journalism."

Sound Publishing president **Josh O'Connor**: O'Connor replied with a copy of an editorial the company's flagship, The Daily Herald in Everett, published Aug. 4, 2020, supporting the act. "Sound Publishing is certainly an advocate and supporter."

Additionally, the committee obtained responses from other publishers and editors in Washington on government support for newspapers:

InvestigateWest's executive director **Jacob Fries** noted many news outlets accepted federal Paycheck Protection Program money during the pandemic. "So, I think news outlets have gotten a bit more used to the idea of government money."

Crosscut managing editor **Mark Baumgarten** said Cascade Public Media, which owns Crosscut and PBS station KCTS-TV, receives public funding. "It's not destroying who we are or what we do. It's not making us any more friendly to our elected leaders."

The Seattle Times' **Alan Fisco**, writing in the Yakima Herald-Republic on Dec. 7, 2021, called for federal assistance. "Yakima and our newspaper industry need federal support to survive and grow again, just like we needed in 1792. The good news is that the need for this support has been recognized by a broad number of enlightened federal legislators."[154]

Back to Table of Contents
Back to study

McChesney offers new plan for news

Author and media critic Robert W. McChesney thinks the commercial model of local news is dead, but he has a plan to breathe new life into it.

"For the first time in U.S. history, most Americans lack access to what used to be considered their birthright," McChesney wrote on the Free Press website on Jan. 25, 2022. McChesney described that birthright as a "well-established, competing and accountable local news media covering their communities and drawing the citizenry into public life."[155]

McChesney has significant credibility on the topic of journalism and democracy, having published several books on the issue.[156]

In 2002, McChesney co-founded Free Press, a national media reform advocacy organization, and served as its president until April 2008. He remains on its board of directors. He has appeared on many news programs as an expert critic exploring threats to American journalism and democracy.

He is proud that his journalism career began in Seattle in the 1980s, where he founded "The Rocket," a rock-and-roll magazine, and published a weekly newspaper, The Seattle Sun. Those experiences, McChesney told the news study committee, fostered his passion "to create effective media institutions that can pay bills and be organized."

His plan to address the local news decline is the Local Journalism Initiative, an effort that he calls superior to proposed legislation because it offers fuel to create more opportunities for reporting local news.

Robert McChesney

"The problem with the Local Journalism Sustainability Act is that it has the government paying the wages for most of the existing reporters for commercial companies," McChesney said. "But that isn't going to create new news media or anything like that."

The foundation of his plan is a fervent belief that our country's founders never envisioned a democracy without journalism. He touts the Thomas Jefferson quote once displayed on the door of the Post-Intelligencer office in Seattle:

> "Were it left to me to decide whether we should have a government without newspapers, or newspapers without a government, I should not hesitate a moment to prefer the latter. But I should mean that every man should receive those papers and be capable of reading them."

McChesney argues that the Local Journalism Initiative would establish a well-funded, competitive, independent, locally based, and uncensored nonprofit news organization in every town, city, and county in the United States.

The plan calls for allocating 0.15% of the country's gross domestic product — $34 billion — to finance nonprofit news operations. Every three years, American adults would have three "votes" to identify which news operations would receive funds. To be eligible for the money, a news operation would be required to make "newsstand" content easily available to audiences for free. No other content supervision by the government would be permitted.

McChesney said the initiative recognizes a civil right to a free press, a necessity to make real the promise of democracy.

He said the plan would give real support to the idea that journalism is a public good and, as the founders believed, fundamental to democracy. Just as education, civil defense, and protection can't necessarily be provided by the marketplace with sufficient quality or quantity, journalism needs government support.

The author is quick to note that the allocation he proposes is just a little more than $100 per person, and that the total is less than the 0.21% of the gross domestic product the government made available to subsidize newspapers through postal discounts in the mid-1800s.

McChesney said response to the initiative has been positive, but he acknowledged that it would be a hard pill to swallow in the United States. He anticipates promoting the plan among civic organizations, including the League of Women Voters, and is encouraging members of the public to support it.

"The nation has been praying for the market and technologies to magically solve the collapse of journalism for nearly two decades and, so far, the prayers have not been answered," he said.

Back to Table of Contents
Back to study

Glossary of terms

Accountability journalism – Work that encompasses fact-checking, explanatory, and investigative reporting, but more generally applies to the journalistic work of holding the powerful accountable. See **watchdog role**, **investigative reporting**.

Aggregator – Someone or something that gathers together materials from a variety of sources, such as a website that collects news stories (Merriam-Webster).

Algorithm – *A set of rules computer coders write to sort and rank search results and other data. The idea is to mimic human decision making to display content that social media users are likely to want to see.*

Beat reporting – A reporter's assigned coverage area. It may be topical, such as an education beat, or geographical, such as a city beat. The reporter regularly monitors from and reports on their assigned beat. The regular monitoring of an area is a type of **accountability journalism**, especially when the beat is a government agency.

Circulation – The average number of copies of a publication. Circulation is not always the same as copies sold, often called paid circulation, since some issues are distributed without cost to the reader. Readership figures are usually higher than circulation figures because of the assumption that a typical copy is read by more than one person.

Daily newspaper – Identified by the Associated Press as one that provides original local news reporting three or more days a week. The study committee includes online-only outlets as newspapers if they provide comprehensive reporting of an area's people, government agencies, schools, and activities.

Disinformation – Deliberately misleading or biased information; manipulated narrative or facts; propaganda. See **misinformation** for the distinction from disinformation.

Fake news – False news stories, often of a sensational nature, created to be widely shared or distributed for the purpose of generating revenue or promoting or discrediting a public figure, political movement, company, etc.

Ghost newspaper – A publication that features editorial content that has been significantly diminished. According to researcher Penelope Muse Abernathy, a ghost newspaper doesn't cover routine government meetings, leaving citizens with little information about important policy issues and decisions.

Hedge fund – An investment partnership that uses high-risk, speculative methods to obtain large, short-term profits.

Investigative reporting – Reporting on topics that people at the center typically don't want revealed. Concealed deliberately or behind facts and circumstances, the information is important to the public's welfare. Investigative reporting is typically time consuming, labor intensive, and expensive. See **accountability journalism**, **watchdog role**.

Misinformation – False information that is spread, regardless of whether there is intent to mislead. See **disinformation** for the distinction from misinformation.

News bureau – An office separate from a main newspaper's newsroom, often in an outlying area, from where journalists report news.

News desert – A community or region that is not covered or served by a daily or weekly newspaper. Researcher Penelope Muse Abernathy reported in 2020 that 200 counties in the United States do not have a local newspaper, and 1,540 counties have only one newspaper, usually a weekly. The news study committee identified one Washington county, Asotin County, where no newspaper is published, although a daily newspaper across the Idaho state line provides coverage.

Opinion or editorial – An unsigned commentary that reflects a newspaper's position on current events or issues.

Opinion or editorial pages – The pages of a newspaper that feature opinions representing the newspaper's point of view, letters to the editor, and signed commentary by other writers, often individuals viewed as experts in their fields.

Paywall – A website feature that enables a publisher to restrict access to content, typically limiting the content to those who pay a subscription.

Pink slime journalism – Sometimes computer generated, sometimes written by outsourced writers, poor quality coverage that appears to be local. In reality, it is often designed to push extreme political points of view and gather data. It is often operated by networks that share content.

Scope of this study – This scope was approved at the 2021 LWVWA Convention: With all we're reading and hearing about the impact of the closing and reduction of local and regional news operations across the nation, what is the situation in Washington state? What, if anything, is happening in the areas of political participation, government oversight, public financing, civic engagement, partisan politics, public health, and other elements that we associate as being fundamental to our democracy and system of government? We also are looking to review various efforts to deal with the reported trends, hoping to garner a better understanding of the problem and potential solutions: legislation, the explosion of nonprofits, partnerships, and philanthropic efforts.

Watchdog role – The press has been conceived of as "fourth estate," or a "counterbalance to powerful institutions in the executive, legislative, and judicial branches in government but also those in the private sector as well," according to "The Watchdog Press in the Doghouse: A Comparative Study of Attitudes about Accountability Journalism, Trust in News, and News Avoidance," International Journal of Press/Politics, 2022.

Back to Table of Contents

Interviews

- Penelope Abernathy, visiting professor, Northwestern University Medill School of Journalism, Media, Integrated Marketing Communications, April 27, 2021
- David Ammons, former Associated Press Capitol bureau political writer, Dec. 1, 2021
- Ofer Amran, assistant professor, Elson S. Floyd College of Medicine, Washington State University, Oct. 27, 2021
- Erica Weintrab Austin, director, Murrow Center for Media and Health Promotion Research, Washington State University, Oct. 20, 2021
- Charlotte Baker, owner and publisher, East Washingtonian and Dayton Chronicle, April 27, 2022
- Matt Baney, city editor, Lewiston Tribune, Feb. 14, 2022
- Mark Baumgarten, managing editor, Crosscut, Jan. 21, 2022
- Chris B. Bennett, CEO of Tiloben Publishing Company, Inc., Feb. 11, 2022
- Cindy Black, executive director, Fix Democracy First, Dec. 9, 2021
- Frank Blethen, publisher of The Seattle Times and CEO of The Seattle Times Company, Feb. 15, 2022
- Jaime Bodden, managing director of Washington State Association of Public Health Officials, Nov. 19, 2021
- Craig Brown, editor, The Columbian, Jan. 28, 2022
- Jonathan Brunt, assistant managing editor for government, The Spokesman-Review, Dec. 8, 2021
- Lisa Bryan, executive editor, Key Peninsula News, Jan. 14, 2022
- Jim Camden, political and state government correspondent, The Spokesman-Review, Dec. 22, 2021
- Will Campbell, Innovation editor, The Columbian, Feb. 4, 2022
- Michael Craw, director Master's in Public Administration program, Evergreen College, Sept. 7, 2021
- Sue Cross, executive director and CEO, Institute for Nonprofit News, Jan. 29, 2022
- Rob Curley, executive editor, The Spokesman-Review, Feb. 15, 2022
- Gayl Curtiss, former advertising executive, The Hacker Group, Jan. 28, 2022
- Nancy Deringer, interim associate dean, director of Washington state 4-H, Washington State University, Nov. 12, 2021
- Michael R. Fancher, president, Washington Coalition for Open Government/former executive editor, The Seattle Times, April 18, 2022
- Bob Ferguson, Washington State Attorney General, Dec. 9, 2021
- Jacob Fries, executive director, InvestigateWest, Jan. 20, 2022
- Jacob Grumbach, assistant professor, University of Washington, Nov. 22, 2021
- Greg Halling, executive editor, Yakima Herald-Republic, March 22, 2022
- Gloria Ibañez, editor, El Sol de Yakima, Feb. 18, 2022
- Ron Judd, executive editor, Cascadia Daily News, Dec. 3, 2021

- Karen Keiser, State Sen. WA 33rd Legislative District, president pro tempore Washington state senate, late 2020
- Derek Kilmer, U.S. Rep., 6th District, March 4, 2022
- Patricia Lantz, president, Gig Harbor Now, Jan. 13, 2022
- Mark Larson, M.D., public health officer, Kittitas County, Nov. 16, 2021
- Emmy Lay, real estate agent, Pierce County, June 17, 2021
- M. David Lee III, executive editor, Crosscut, Jan. 21, 2022
- Bob Lutz, M.D., Asotin County public health officer, former Spokane County public health officer, Nov. 5, 2021
- Brenda Mann Harrison, journalism development director, Everett Herald, Feb. 3, 2022
- Robert W. McChesney, emeritus professor, University of Illinois, media critic and author, April 18, 2022
- Dermot Murphy, assistant professor, Department of Finance, University of Illinois, Nov. 2, 2021
- Josh O'Connor, president, Sound Publishing, Black Press, Jan. 10, 2022, Jan 14, 2022.
- Fred Obee, executive director, Washington Newspaper Publishers Association, Sept. 24, 2021
- Betty Oppenheimer, communications specialist, Jamestown S'Klallam Tribe, Feb. 3, 2022
- Stephanie Pedersen, president and editor, The (Tacoma) News Tribune, March 23, 2022
- Mike Pellicciotti, Washington State Treasurer, Jan. 21, 2022
- Jerry Pettit, county auditor, Kittitas County, Feb. 18, 2022
- Paul Queary, editor and publisher, The Washington Observer and Washington State Wire, Jan. 13, 2022
- Travis N. Ridout, Thomas S. Foley Distinguished Professor of Government and Public Policy, Washington State University, Feb. 1, 2022
- Lee Shaker, associate professor, Department of Communication, Portland State University, Nov. 2, 2021
- Benjamin Shors, associate professor (CT), chair Dept. of Journalism & Media Production, Washington State University, July 20, 2022
- Danny Stusser, executive director, The Journal of Olympia, Lacey and Tumwater (JOLT), Jan. 19, 2022
- David Syre, owner, Cascadia Daily News, Dec. 3, 2021
- Rowland Thompson, executive director, Allied Daily Newspapers of Washington, Dec. 3, 2021
- Jenny Wellman, treasurer, Gig Harbor Now, Jan. 13, 2022.
- Sandra Williams, editor and publisher, The Black Lens, March 2, 2022
- Matt Winters, editor and publisher of the Chinook Observer, Jul. 22, 2022
- David Zeeck, former executive editor and publisher of The News Tribune, Bellingham Herald, and The Olympian, Nov. 4, 2021

Back to Table of Contents

Charts and graphs

Figure 1   Do You Live in a News Desert? - UNC Hussman School of Journalism and Media 6
Figure 2   Comparing two newspapers – News study committee 11
Figure 3   Newsroom staffing declines – U.S. Senate Committee report on local news 12
Figure 4   Page count decreases – News study committee 13
Figure 5   Washington daily newspapers – News study committee 14
Figure 6   News deserts - the demographics – Medill Local News Initiative 17
Figure 7   U.S counties without a newspaper – UNC Hussman School of Journalism 18
Figure 8   Washington statehouse reporters reduced by half – Pew Research Center 23
Figure 9   Majority of Americans get news on digital devices – Pew Research Center 27
Figure 10   Internet surpassed newspapers as a source – Pew Rearch Center 28
Figure 11   Newspaper Advertising Revenue, 1950-2014 – Newspaper Association of America 29
Figure 12   Advertising and Circulation Revenue, Newspaper Industry – News Media Alliance 31
Figure 13   Chatham Asset Management Newspapers in Washington 33
Figure 14   About Half of Americans Get News on Social Media – Pew Research Center 35
Figure 15   Half of Users Get News from Facebook – Pew Research Center 36
Figure 16   Voter Participation in February County Special Elections, News study committee 42
Figure 17   Nonprofit News in Washington – News study committee 60
Figure 18   How good is your news? – UNC Hussman School of Journalism and Media 82
Figure 19   Washington Newspapers in 2004 and 2022 – News study committee 83
Figure 20   Newspapers by County – News study committee 89
Figure 21   Sound Publishing Newspapers 2022 – News study committee 92
Figure 22   Washington Voting Data, 2008 to 2021 – News study committee 100
Figure 23   Proposed Legislation – News study committee 113

Back to Table of Contents

Study participants

Study committee

Dee Anne Finken, co-chair, joined the League of Women Voters in 1986. At the time, she was on maternity leave from The Fresno Bee, where she was a staff reporter for 12 years. Also a longtime freelancer for The Oregonian in Portland, she directed the journalism program at Clark College before retiring in 2018.

Delores Irwin, co-chair, was a newspaper reporter at Southern California newspapers, including the Orange County Register. She also identifies as a former bureaucrat for a public hospital, a city, and a community college district, all in Southern California. She is the former League president in Kittitas County.

Sally Carpenter Hale is a retired bureau chief and account director who spent 40 years with The Associated Press in Texas, Oregon, Pennsylvania, and New Jersey. She was the founding president of the Pennsylvania Freedom of Information Coalition and served on the boards of the Pennsylvania NewsMedia Association and PNA Foundation. She currently freelances as a travel writer/photographer with a focus on wine tourism.

Linda Hughes is a member of the League of Women Voters Bellingham-Whatcom County. Her longtime interest in journalism and the news led her to join this study. She retired from employment in community college student services, and later, direct service and then management in a federally funded employment and training program. She has a long history of community involvement.

Joanne M. Lisosky, who holds a Ph.D., had a career in multimedia journalism, then taught journalism and advised student media at Pacific Lutheran University for more than 20 years. Her tenure at PLU also included three Fulbright Awards teaching journalism in Uganda, Azerbaijan, and Trinidad/Tobago. Her book, "War on Words: Who Should Protect Journalists?" was co-authored with a former PLU student.

Carol Rikerd joined the League about five years ago when she represented another civic organization at a LWV event. She has been an avid reader of local newspapers since age 9. Retired from federal employment, she now tends the perennial border gardens she's been building for several decades.

Lauren Snider's career was in academic biomedical research, including 27 years at Fred Hutchinson Cancer Research Center. Snider, a Ph.D., holds high regard for the value of accurate, reliable, and accessible information to drive decision making. She is a member of the Seattle-King County League of Women Voters.

Lyn Whitley earned a B.A. in journalism at the University of North Carolina at Chapel Hill. She worked for 10 years covering local news in North Carolina and Alaska before moving to corporate public relations and advertising in the healthcare industry and later in commercial banking for 35 years.

Sharon Wilhelm, a member of the League of Women Voters of Tacoma-Pierce County since 2016, is a nonjournalist but is an avid reader and subscriber to one national and two local newspapers. She retired from nonprofit hospital and community service work in 2015. She has served in volunteer capacities as a board member or officer in several civic and public service organizations.

Amanda Clark was an editor for 40 years, working on publications ranging from textbooks and technical users' guides to academic journals and newsletters. Though never a journalist, she is an avid reader and supporter of national and local news. She is also an active member of the League of Women Voters, and has served as president of the Seattle-King County League and on the Washington League board of directors.

Dee Ann Kline, state board liaison, joined the LWV in 2016 when she retired from a career in health care. She has been serving as LWVWA treasurer since July 2021. She is active in LWV Mason County, where she is the Voter

Services Chair and a member of the four-person Leadership Team. She also updates the Mason County LWV website and publishes their Voter newsletter.

Kelly Hale McNabb is a freelance graphic designer, business owner, and Six Sigma-certified black belt. She's an active volunteer in her community in Salem, Ore., and has three children who keep her busy.

Reading committee

Judie Stanton joined the League in 1981 and has served in several capacities in her local League. In addition to her involvement in numerous community activities, she has served in local government as an elected member of the Vancouver School Board, Fire District 5 Commission, and as a Clark County commissioner. Most recently she has become a master gardener and enjoys helping with the Answer Clinic.

Lucy Copass, a 50+ year member of the LWV, has chaired studies and written testimony at the local, state, and national level. In her non-League life, Copass was an assistant editor for World Book Encyclopedia and a consultant to government agencies on their public involvement programs. She loves to grow vegetables in her garden on the North Olympic Peninsula and to hike in the high country.

Carolyn Maddux, who joined the League two years ago, reported for her local newspaper in high school. Originally an English teacher, she spent most of her career working at the Shelton-Mason County Journal under legendary editor Henry Gay and, later, Charles Gay, as beat reporter and managing editor. After retiring, she taught English at Olympic College Shelton and continues teaching creative writing.

Technical review

William Dietrich is a novelist, nonfiction writer, journalist, assistant professor, and winner of a Pulitzer Prize. A graduate of Western Washington University, Dietrich spent a year at Harvard University in the Nieman fellowship program for journalists and was a fellow at the Woods Hole Marine Biological Laboratory. As a staff writer at The Seattle Times, he was a member of a reporting team that won a Pulitzer Prize for its coverage of the Exxon Valdez oil spill in Alaska. He also serves on the board of directors of the nonprofit Salish Current.

Brier Dudley is the editor of The Seattle Times' Save the Free Press Initiative. At the Times since 1998, he previously covered technology and was a member of the newspaper's editorial board. A graduate of Whitman College, he completed an Asia Pacific Journalism fellowship at the East-West Center, studied film making, and was a staff member at The News Tribune and the Yakima Herald-Republic.

Benjamin Shors is chair of the Department of Journalism and Media Production at the Edward R. Murrow College of Communication at Washington State University, where he is a career track associate professor. An award-winning journalist and filmmaker specializing in public-interest reporting in the Pacific Northwest, Shors also is project manager for the Murrow News Service, which provides local, regional, and national stories reported and written by Murrow College journalism students. Shors earned his master's degree in journalism from the University of Montana and was a fellow with the International Center for Journalists.

Peggy Watt is an associate professor of journalism at Western Washington University, where she teaches media law and reporting. She earned a master's degree from Stanford University, where she wrote her thesis on traditional journalism's role in new media. Early in her career, Watt worked as a reporter and editor at community newspapers in Washington and California and then covered Silicon Valley, writing and editing for various publications including PC World. She also serves on the board of the Washington Coalition for Open Government.

Back to Table of Contents

Endnotes

1 Abernathy, Penelope Muse, "The News Landscape in 2020: Transformed and Diminished," The Expanding News Desert, University of North Carolina, Hussman School of Journalism and Media, 2020, https://www.usnewsdeserts.com/reports/news-deserts-and-ghost-newspapers-will-local-news-survive/the-news-landscape-in-2020-transformed-and-diminished/.

2 "What makes journalism different than other forms of communication?" The American Press Institute, 2022, https://www.americanpressinstitute.org/journalism-essentials/what-is-journalism/makes-journalism-different-forms-communication/.

3 Napoli , Philip, and Jessica Mahone, "Local newspapers are suffering, but they're still (by far) the most significant journalism producers in their communities," Nieman Lab, 9 Sept. 2019, https://www.niemanlab.org/2019/09/local-newspapers-are-suffering-but-theyre-still-by-far-the-most-significant-journalism-producers-in-their-communities/.

4 Waldman , Steven, and the Working Group on Information Needs of Communities, the Federal Communications Commission, "The Information Needs of Communities: The changing media landscape in a broadband age," July 2011, https://transition.fcc.gov/osp/inc-report/The_Information_Needs_of_Communities.pdf.

5 Benton, Josh, "The Wall Street Journal joins The New York Times in the 2 million digital subscriber club," Nieman Lab, 10 Feb. 2020, https://www.niemanlab.org/2020/02/the-wall-street-journal-joins-the-new-york-times-in- the-2-million-digital-subscriber-club/.

6 Waldman and the Working Group on Information Needs of Communities, the Federal Communications Commission, "The Information Needs of Communities: The changing media landscape in a broadband age."

7 McChesney, Robert, and John Nichols, "To Protect and Extend Democracy, Recreate Local News Media," FreePress.net, 25 Jan. 2022, https://www.freepress.net/sites/default/files/2022-03/to_protect_democracy_recreate_local_news_media_final.pdf.

8 U.S. Senate Committee on Commerce, Science and Transportation, "Local Journalism: America's Most Trusted News Source Threatened," page 19, October 2020, https://www.cantwell.senate.gov/news/press-releases/senate-commerce-committee-minority-report-calls-unfair-practices-by-tech-companies-a-threat-to-local-news.

9 "A Deep Cut: Seattle Times to Eliminate 200 Jobs," National Press Photographers Association newsletter, 7 Apr. 2008, https://nppa.org/news/1433.

10 Long, Katherine Khashimova, "As advertising dries up amid coronavirus shutdown, Washington news outlets lay off staff." The Seattle Times, 26 Mar. 2020, https://www.seattletimes.com/business/local-business/as-advertising-dries-up-amid-coronavirus-shutdown-washington-news-outlets-lay-off-staff/.

11 Howard, Marcus E., "How Journalists and the Public Shape Our Democracy," Georgia Humanities Council, 2019, https://www.georgiahumanities.org/wp-content/uploads/2019/03/MediaGuide_Web.pdf.

12 Abernathy, "The News Landscape in 2020: Transformed and Diminished," The Expanding News Desert, 2020, https://www.usnewsdeserts.com/reports/news-deserts-and-ghost-newspapers-will-local-news-survive/the-news-landscape-in-2020-transformed-and-diminished/.

13 Halling, Greg, "From the Editor: Yakima Herald-Republic invests in the future, to move to 3 days a week in print," Yakima Herald-Republic, 1 Feb. 2022, https://www.yakimaherald.com/news/local/from-the-editor-yakima-herald-republic-invests-in-the-future-to-move-to-3-days/article_461d2b2e-323e-5080-ba46-d0631219c970.html.

14 Abernathy, Penelope Muse, "The State of Local News in 2022," Northwestern University, Medill School of Journalism and Media, .https://localnewsinitiative.northwestern.edu/research/state-of-local-news/report/.

15Report For America, https://www.reportforamerica.org/newsrooms/the-news-tribune-in-partnership-with-the-olympian-the-bellingham-herald-and-the-tri-city-herald/.

16 thevanished.org

17 Queary, Paul, "Evicted: The Incredible Shrinking State House Press," Post Alley, 7 Apr. 2021, https://www.postalley.org/2021/04/07/evicted-the-incredible-shrinking-state-house-press/.

18 Randels, Chris, Soundside radio show, KUOW, 94.9 FM, 22 Mar. 2022.

19 "Okanogan County Watch Recognized With Key Award," Washington Coalition for Open Government, May 2018, https://www.washcog.org/newsletter/okanogan-county-watch-key-award.

20 Fisco, Alan, "How is it that the Yakima Herald-Republic and El Sol are at Risk?" Yakima Herald-Republic, 7 Dec. 2021, https://www.yakimaherald.com/opinion/free_press/yfp/how-is-it-that-yakima-herald-republic-and-el-sol-are-at-risk/article_93e7877e-2aec-5c5b-880a-3b4eb9349ac9.html.

21 Owen, Lauren Hazard, "Expensive, boring, and wrong," Nieman Lab, 28 Oct. 2021, https://www.niemanlab.org/2021/10/expensive-boring-and-wrong-here-are-all-the-news-publications-people-canceled-and-why/#s.

22 Nieman Lab staff, "Cancel culture," Nieman Lab, 28 Oct. 2021, https://www.niemanlab.org/2021/10/cancel-culture-why-do-people-cancel-news-subscriptions-we-asked-they-answered/.

23 "Key findings about the online news landscape in America," Pew Research Center, 11 Sept. 2019, https://www.pewresearch.org/fact-tank/2019/09/11/key-findings-about-the-online-news-landscape-in-america/.

24 Shearer, Elisa, "More than eight-in-ten Americans get news from digital devices," 12 Jan. 2021, https://www.pewresearch.org/fact-tank/2021/01/12/more-than-eight-in-ten-americans-get-news-from-digital-devices/.

25 Sridhar , Shrihari and Srinivasaraghavan Sriram, "Is online newspaper advertising cannibalizing print advertising?" 5 Oct. 2015, https://link.springer.com/article/10.1007/s11129-015-9160-3.

26 "Only 5% of web users would pay for online news, reports survey," The Guardian, 21 Sept. 2009, https://www.theguardian.com/media/pda/2009/sep/21/paid-content-newspapers-online-news.

27 Parr, Sam, "Newsweek in 1995: Why the Internet Will Fail," The Hustle, 21 Dec. 2015, https://thehustle.co/clifford-stoll-why-the-internet-will-fail/#:~:text=In%20his%20article%2C%20Stoll%20claimed%20that%20the%20internet,or%20portable.%20Also%2C%20it%20is%20different%20and%20scary.%E2%80%9D.

28 "Newspapers Fact Sheet," Pew Research Center, 29 June 2021, https://www.pewresearch.org/journalism/fact-sheet/newspapers/.

29 "Share of newspaper advertising revenue coming from digital advertising," 29 June 2021, Pew Research Center, https://www.pewresearch.org/journalism/chart/sotnm-newspapers-%age-of-newspaper-advertising-revenue-coming-from-digital/.

30 Shepardson, David, "U.S. agency needs new powers to protect local news industry, senator says," Reuters, 27 Oct. 2020, https://www.reuters.com/article/us-usa-media-congress-idCAKBN27C12Y.

31 "State of the News Media," Pew Research Center, 15 June 2016, https://www.pewresearch.org/wp-content/uploads/sites/8/2016/06/state-of-the-news-media-report-2016-final.pdf.

32 Edmonds, Rick, "Newspaper declines accelerate, latest Pew Research finds, other sectors healthier," Poynter, 15 June 2016, https://www.poynter.org/business-work/2016/newspaper-declines-accelerate-latest-pew-research-finds-other-sectors-healthier/.

33 Angelucci, Charles, et al., "Media Competition and News Diets, 13 Feb. 2020, https://spire.sciencespo.fr/hdl:/2441/4ec86lkes59hv9tfv77ld1p5fr/resources/2020-angelucci-cage-sinkinson-media-competition-and-news-diets.pdf.

34 Helmore, Edward, "Fears for future of American journalism as hedge funds flex power," The Guardian, 21 June 2021, https://www.theguardian.com/media/2021/jun/21/us-newspapers-journalism-industry-hedge-funds.

35 O'Connell , Jonathan, and Emma Brown, "A hedge fund's 'mercenary' strategy: Buy newspapers, slash jobs, sell the buildings," The Washington Post, 11 Feb. 2019, https://www.washingtonpost.com/business/economy/a-hedge-funds-mercenary-strategy-buy-newspapers-slash-jobs-sell-the-buildings/2019/02/11/f2c0c78a-1f59-11e9-8e21-59a09ff1e2a1_story.html#:~:text=A%20hedge%20fund%E2%80%99s%20%E2%80%98mercenary%E2%80%99%20strategy%3A%20Buy%20newspapers%2C%20slash,known%20for%20its%20drastic%20cost%20cuts.%20%28Andrew%20Harrer%2FBloomberg%29.

36 Sullivan, Margaret, "Is this strip-mining or journalism? 'Sobs, gasps, expletives' over latest Denver Post layoffs," The Washington Post, 15 Mar. 2018, https://www.washingtonpost.com/lifestyle/style/is-this-strip-mining-or-journalism-sobs-gasps-expletives-over-latest-denver-post-layoffs/2018/03/15/d05abc5a-287e-11e8-874b-d517e912f125_story.html.

37 Chakradhar, Shraddha, "'An immediate drop in content': A new study shows what happens when big companies take over local news," Nieman Lab, 20 Apr. 2022, https://www.niemanlab.org/2022/04/an-immediate-drop-in-content-a-new-study-shows-what-happens-when-big-companies-take-over-local-news/.

38 Edmonds, Rick, "Chatham Asset Management, a hedge fund, has won the auction to buy the McClatchy newspaper chain," Poynter, 12 July 2020, https://www.poynter.org/locally/2020/hedge-fund-chatham-asset-management-buy-the-mcclatchy-newspaper-chain/.

39 Sato, Mike, "Bellingham Herald news reporters opt to unionize, for the cause of 'robust local news,' Salish Current, 18 Dec. 2020, https://salish-current.org/2021/01/14/bellingham-herald-news-reporters-opt-to-unionize-for-the-cause-of-robust-local-news/.

40 Frederic Remington, Wikipedia, May 14, 2022, https://en.wikipedia.org/wiki/Frederic_Remington#In_Cuba.

41 Greenemeier, Larry, "You Can't Handle the Truth — At Least on Twitter," Scientific American, 8 Mar. 2018, https://www.scientificamerican.com/article/you-cant-handle-the-truth-at-least-on-twitter/.

42 Shearer , Elisa, and Amy Mitchell, "News Use Across Social Media Platforms in 2020," Pew Research Center, 12 Jan. 2021, https://www.pewresearch.org/journalism/2021/01/12/news-use-across-social-media-platforms-in-2020/#:~:text=About%20half%20of%20U.S.%20adults%20%2853%25%29%20say%20they,Research%20Center%20survey%20conducted%20Aug.%2031-Sept.%207%2C%202020.

43 https://mediactive.newscollab.org

44 "Disinformation in the media: Two ASU journalism experts weigh in," ASU News, 17 Aug. 2020, https://news.asu.edu/20200817-disinformation-media-two-asu-journalism-experts-weigh.

45 Bengani, Priyanjana, "Hundreds of 'pink slime' local news outlets are distributing algorithmic stories and conservative talking points," Tow Center for Digital Journalism, 18 Dec. 2019, https://www.cjr.org/tow_center_reports/hundreds-of-pink-slime-local-news-outlets-are-distributing-algorithmic-stories-conservative-talking-points.php.

46 Bengani, Priyanjana, "As election looms, a network of mysterious 'pink slime' local news outlets nearly triples," Columbia Journalism Review, 4 Aug. 2020, https://www.cjr.org/analysis/as-election-looms-a-network-of-mysterious-pink-slime-local-news-outlets-nearly-triples-in-size.php.

47 Graham, Jennifer, "Understanding 'pink slime journalism' and what it reveals about conservatives and liberals," DeseretNews, 7 Sept. 2020, https://www.deseret.com/indepth/2020/9/7/21409053/understanding-pink-slime-journalism-and-what-it-reveals-about-conservatives-and-liberals.

48 Coppins, McKay, "The Billion-Dollar Disinformation Campaign To Re-elect The President," The Atlantic, 20 Feb. 2020, https://www.theatlantic.com/magazine/archive/2020/03/the-2020-disinformation-war/605530/.

49 Bengani, Priyanjana, 14 Oct. 2021, https://www.cjr.org/tow_center_reports/community-newsmaker-metric-media-local-news.php.

50 Metric Media, https://metricmedianews.com/.

51 Metric Media, 28 May 2022, https://mediabiasfactcheck.com/metric-media/.

52 Anderson, Monica, and Skye Toor, "How social media users have discussed sexual harassment since #MeToo went viral," Pew Research Center, 11 Oct. 2018, https://www.pewresearch.org/fact-tank/2018/10/11/how-social-media-users-have-discussed-sexual-harassment-since-metoo-went-viral/.

53 Brown, Heather, et al., "The Role of Social Media in the Arab Uprisings," Pew Research Center, 28 Nov. 2012, https://www.pewresearch.org/journalism/2012/11/28/role-social-media-arab-uprisings/.

54 Nelson, Jacob L., "A Twitter tightrope without a net," Columbia Journalism Review, 2 Dec. 2021, https://www.cjr.org/tow_center_reports/newsroom-social-media-policies.php.

55 Popik, Barry, 19 June 2010 entry, https://www.barrypopik.com/index.php/new_york_city/entry/if_your_mother_says_she_loves_you_check_it_out.

56 Society of Professional Journalists Code of Ethics, https://www.spj.org/ethicscode.asp.

57 Rubado , Meghan E. of Cleveland State University and Jennings , Jay T. of the University of Texas, "Political Consequences of the Endangered Local Watchdog: Newspaper Decline and Mayoral Elections in the United States," Urban Affairs Review, 3 Apr. 2019, https://journals.sagepub.com/doi/abs/10.1177/1078087419838058?journalCode=uarb.

58 Holder, Sarah, "When Local Newsrooms Shrink, Fewer Candidates Run for Mayor," Bloomberg, 11 Apr. 2019, https://www.bloomberg.com/news/articles/2019-04-11/as-local-newspapers-shrink-so-do-voters-choices.

59 Tobitt, Charlotte, "Newspaper circulation and voter turnout: Absence of journalism in some areas potentially 'catastrophic,'" PressGazette, 6 Oct. 2020, https://pressgazette.co.uk/uk-gov-report-finds-direct-link-between-local-newspaper-circulation-and-voter-turnout-absence-of-journalism-in-some-areas-potentially-catastrophic/.

60 Whatcom County sample ballot, 3 Nov. 2015, https://whatcomcounty.us/DocumentCenter/View/12532/110315-Sample-Ballot?bidId=.

61 Dudley, Brier, "Democracy is at stake when local news sources decline," Yakima Herald-Republic, 7 Dec. 2021, https://www.yakimaherald.com/opinion/free_press/yfp/democracy-is-at-stake-when-local-news-sources-decline/article_e9e73361-6ed6-55fa-ab4b-b7ffb96e3f5c.html.

62 Darr, Joshua, "Local News Coverage is Declining – And That Could Be Bad for American Politics," FiveThirtyEight, 2 June 2021, https://fivethirtyeight.com/features/local-news-coverage-is-declining-and-that-could-be-bad-for-american-politics/.

63 Walsh, Dylan, "Without a Local Newspaper, Americans Pay Less Attention to Local Politics," Yale Insights, 23 Sept. 2021, https://insights.som.yale.edu/insights/without-local-newspaper-americans-pay-less-attention-to-local-politics.

64 Hayes , Danny, and Jennifer Lawless, "News Hole: The Demise of Local Journalism and Political Engagement," Cambridge University Press, 2021, https://academic.oup.com/poq/advance-article-abstract/doi/10.1093/poq/nfac005/6555522?redirectedFrom=fulltext&login=false.

65 Mathews, Nick, University of Minnesota, "Life in a news desert: The perceived impact of a newspaper closure on community members," 28 Sept. 2020, https://journals.sagepub.com/doi/10.1177/1464884920957885.

66 Barthel, Michael, et. al., "Civic Engagement Strongly Tied to Local News Habits," Pew Research Center, 1 Nov. 2016, https://assets.pewresearch.org/wp-content/uploads/sites/13/2016/11/02163924/PJ_2016.11.02_Civic-Engagement_FINAL.pdf.

67 Dudley, Brier, "Democracy is at stake when local news sources decline," Yakima Herald-Republic, 7 Dec. 2021, https://www.yakimaherald.com/opinion/free_press/yfp/democracy-is-at-stake-when-local-news-sources-decline/article_e9e73361-6ed6-55fa-ab4b-b7ffb96e3f5c.html.

68 Godfrey, Elaine, "What We Lost When Gannett Came to Town," The Atlantic, 5 Oct. 2021, https://www.editorandpublisher.com/stories/what-we-lost-when-gannett-came-to-town,205164.

69 Branswell, Helen, "As towns lose their newspapers, disease detectives are left flying blind," STAT, 20 Mar. 2018, https://www.statnews.com/2018/03/20/news-deserts-infectious-disease/.

70 Harris, Lauren, "The decline of local newsrooms could make it harder for us to detect the next disease outbreak," Columbia Journalism Review, 7 Oct. 2020, https://www.cjr.org/business_of_news/the-decline-of-local-newsrooms-could-make-it-harder-for-us-to-detect-the-next-disease-outbreak.php.

71 Hendrickson, Clara, "Critical in a public health crisis, COVID-19 has hit local newsrooms hard," Brookings Institute, 8 Apr. 2020, https://www.brookings.edu/blog/fixgov/2020/04/08/critical-in-a-public-health-crisis-covid-19-has-hit-local-newsrooms-hard/.

72 Smith , Hedrick, Salish Current fundraiser, 17 Mar. 2022, Bellingham, Wash.

73 Folkenflik, David, "How The L.A. Times Broke the Bell Corruption Story," NPR.org, 24 Sept. 2010, https://www.npr.org/2010/09/24/130108851/how-the-l-a-times-broke-the-bell-corruption-story.

74 Gottlieb , Jeff, and Ruben Vives, "D.A. investigating why Bell council members get nearly $100,000 a year for a part-time job," Los Angeles Times, 24 June 2010, https://www.latimes.com/local/la-me-0624-maywood-20100624-story.html.

75 Folkenflik, "How The L.A. Times Broke the Bell Corruption Story."

76 Gao, Pengie, et al., "Financing Dies in Darkness? The Impact of Newspaper Closures on Public Finance," Hutchins Center on Fiscal and Monetary Policy, Sept. 2018, https://www.brookings.edu/research/financing-dies-in-darkness-the-impact-of-newspaper-closures-on-public-finance/.

77 Heese, Jonas, et al., "When the local newspaper leaves town: the effect of newspaper closures on corporate misconduct," Journal of Financial Economics, 9 Aug. 2021, https://papers.ssrn.com/sol3/papers.cfm?abstract_id=3889039.

78 Knight Foundation, "Local news and the new media landscape," 5 Apr. 2018, https://knightfoundation.org/reports/local-tv-news-and-the-new-media-landscape/.

79 Fisco, "How is it that Yakima Herald-Republic and El Sol are at risk?"

80 Miracle, Sharon, "Pilot explores new press funding models," Yakima Herald-Republic, 7 Dec. 2021, https://www.yakimaherald.com/opinion/free_press/yfp/pilot-project-explores-models-to-tackle-challenges-facing-free-press-in-the-yakima-valley-and/article_8a1a361f-cee4-55be-940b-83b713774a42.html?utm_medium=social&utm_source=email&utm_campaign=user-share.

81 Halling, Greg,"An essential news team at the YHR will make the community stronger," Yakima Herald-Republic, 23 Jan. 2022, https://www.yakimaherald.com/opinion/column-an-essential-news-team-at-the-yhr-will-make-the-community-stronger/article_9c75bbce-4284-5464-97db-07089f8f02d8.html.

82 Yang, Nu, "2020 E&P Publisher of the Year Frank Blethen, Seattle Times," Editor & Publisher, 2 Nov. 2020, https://www.editorandpublisher.com/stories/2020-ep-publisher-of-the-year-frank-blethen-seattle-times,178554.

83 Pedersen, Stephanie, "The News Tribune wants to expand its education coverage. But first, let me tell you why," The News Tribune, 31 Oct. 2020, https://www.thenewstribune.com/news/local/article246851457.html.

84 The News Tribune Coronavirus Reporting Fund, The News Tribune, https://givebutter.com/thenewstribune.

85 The News Tribune Education Reporting Fund, The News Tribune, https://givebutter.com/newstrib.

86 Report for America Annual Report, 2020, https://d3b9fkm0acb8s3.cloudfront.net/wp-content/uploads/2021/03/Report-for-America_Local-Sustainability-Annual-Report-2021.pdf.

87 Institute for Nonprofit News, https://inn.org/.

88 "Knight investment in INN will catalyze the growth of nonprofit news," Institute for Nonprofit News, 19 Sept. 2022, https://inn.org/news/knight-investment-in-inn-will-catalyze-the-growth-of-nonprofit-news-2/?fbclid=IwAR0OSXU0NknFbuJ_SVMs7V_p9WFZPENTgnnMBy28wvjhfOH6rj-cUOPJSVE

89 "Local Journalism: America's Most Trusted News Source Threatened," U.S. Senate Committee on Commerce, Science, and Transportation, October 2020, https://www.cantwell.senate.gov/news/press-releases/senate-commerce-committee-minority-report-calls-unfair-practices-by-tech-companies-a-threat-to-local-news.

90 Shepardson, David, "U.S. agency needs new powers to protect local news industry, senator says," Reuters, 27 Oct. 2020, https://www.reuters.com/article/us-usa-media-congress/u-s-agency-needs-new-powers-to-protect-local-news-industry-senator-says-idUSKBN27C12Y.

91 Coster, Helen, "Google, Facebook pledged millions for local news – was it enough?" amNY, 20 June 2021, https://www.amny.com/news/google-facebook-pledged-millions-for-local-news-was-it-enough/.

92 Dudley, Brier, "Q&A on Microsoft's expanding journalism initiative," Yakima Herald-Republic, 3 Dec. 2021, https://www.yakimaherald.com/q-a-on-microsoft-s-expanding-journalism-initiative/article_2739e371-08e4-5866-8bf3-a17e64f066b1.html.

93 Dudley, Brier, "Democracy is at stake when local news sources decline," Yakima Herald-Republic, 7 Dec. 2021, https://www.yakimaherald.com/opinion/free_press/yfp/democracy-is-at-stake-when-local-news-sources-decline/article_e9e73361-6ed6-55fa-ab4b-b7ffb96e3f5c.html.

94 Dudley, "Expanding."

95 "The GNI Ad Transformation Lab: Helping Black and Latino News Publishers Grow Digital Revenue," Editor & Publisher, 25 July 2021, https://www.editorandpublisher.com/stories/the-gni-ad-transformation-lab-helping-black-and-latino-news-publishers-grow-digital-revenue,198595.

96 "2022 GNI Ad Transformation Lab Is Underway," Association of Alternative Media, 7 Feb. 2022, https://aan.org/aan/2022-gni-ad-transformation-lab/.

97 Jacob, Mark, "Google Gives Boost to Medill's Subscriber Index as More News Outlets Prepare to Join," LocalNewsIni, Northwestern/Medill Local News Initiative, 27 Jan. 2022, https://localnewsinitiative.northwestern.edu/posts/2022/01/27/google-index-partnership/index.html.

98 Brown, Campbell, "Facebook Helps Local News Publishers Build Digital Subscriptions," Meta Journalism Project, 27 Feb. 2018, https://www.facebook.com/journalismproject/facebook-local-news-digital-subscriptions.

99 Ortutay, Barbara, "Facebook to invest $300 million in news, focusing on local," ABC News, 15 Jan. 2019, https://abcnews.go.com/Technology/wireStory/facebook-invest-300-local-news-initiatives-60384780.

100 Fischer, Sara, "Scoop: Meta officially cuts funding for U.S news publishers," Axios, 28 July 2022, https://www.axios.com/2022/07/28/meta-publishers-news-funding-cut.

101 Sen. Maria Cantwell news release, 22 July 2021, https://www.cantwell.senate.gov/news/press-releases/cantwell-kelly-wyden-introduce-legislation-to-revive-sustain-trusted-local-news.

102 Rep. Dan Newhouse news release, 16 June 2021, https://newhouse.house.gov/media-center/press-releases/newhouse-kirkpatrick-introduce-local-journalism-sustainability-act.

103 Franklin, Tim, news conference 29 June 2022, to release latest study from Northwestern University's Medill School of Journalism titled "Struggling Communities Hardest Hit by Decline in Local Journalism."

104 Public hearing on SB5526, Washington Senate Business, Financial Services & Trade Committee, 20 Jan. 2022, https://tvw.org/video/senate-business-financial-services-trade-committee-2022011292/?eventID=2022011292.

105 Tracking Subsidies, Promoting Accountability in Economic Development, Good Jobs First, www.goodjobsfirst.org/showusthesubsidizedjobs.

106 Ingram, Mathew, "Government funding for journalism: necessary evil or just evil?" Columbia Journalism Review, 24 Jan. 2020, https://www.cjr.org/the_media_today/government-funding-journalism.php.

107 The Passage of the Public Broadcasting Act of 1967, 14 Feb. 2017, The Byrd Center Blog, https://www.byrdcenter.org/blog/the-passage-of-the-public-broadcasting-act-of-1967.

108 Ballotpedia, https://ballotpedia.org/PBS.

109 "Turner Broadcasting System, Inc., v. FCC," FindLaw.com, https://caselaw.findlaw.com/us-supreme-court/512/622.html.

110 "Media Cross-Ownership in the United States," Wikipedia, https://en.wikipedia.org/wiki/Media_cross-ownership_in_the_United_States.

111 Frank Blethen, "Save the Free Press initiative: A public service of The Seattle Times," 20 Dec. 2019, https://www.seattletimes.com/business/local-business/save-the-free-press-initiative-a-public-service-of-the-seattle-times/.

112 The United States Postal Service: An American History, 2020, https://about.usps.com/publications/pub100.pdf.

113 Cowan , Geoffrey, and David Westphal, "Public Policy and Funding the News," USC Annenberg School for Communication & Journalism, January 2010, https://fundingthenews.usc.edu/report/.

114 "The Decline of American Journalism – Robert McChesney," the Analysis.news, 9 Dec. 2020, https://theanalysis.news/the-decline-of-american-journalism-robert-mcchesney/.

115 McChesney, "To Protect and Extend Democracy, Recreate Local Media," 2022.

116 The Associated Press, "New Orleans' Times-Picayune to drop daily circulation," New Haven Register, 24 May 2012, https://www.nhregister.com/news/article/New-Orleans-Times-Picayune-to-drop-daily-11452089.php.

117 Edmonds, Rick, "A Q&A with Tampa Bay Times chairman and CEO Paul Tash about the Times' print reduction," Poynter, 30 Mar. 2020, https://www.poynter.org/business-work/2020/a-qa-with-tampa-bay-times-chairman-and-ceo-paul-tash-about-the-times-print-reduction/.

118 "Columbian to drop Monday print edition, make other changes," The Columbian, 6 Dec. 2019, https://www.columbian.com/news/2019/dec/06/columbian-to-drop-monday-print-edition-make-other-changes/.

119 "Kitsap Sun changing schedule of print newspaper production," Kitsap Sun, 13 Jan. 2022, https://news.yahoo.com/kitsap-sun-changing-schedule-print-183828967.html?fr=yhssrp_catchall.

120 Meyers, Donald W., "Census data shows Latinos now make up more than half of Yakima County's population," Yakima Herald-Republic, 17 Aug. 2021, https://www.yakimaherald.com/news/local/census-data-shows-latinos-now-make-up-more-than-half-of-yakima-countys-population/article_6ee0b9f7-b01c-5d4f-a54e-7f5c6310b0b2.html.

121 Tracy, Marc, "Regional newspapers see salvation in online subscription growth," The Seattle Times, 12 Feb. 2022, https://www.seattletimes.com/business/regional-newspapers-see-salvation-in-online-subscription-growth/.

122 Jacob, Mark, "Small publishers have longer runway to digital but they still need to take off," E&P, 9 Sept. 2021, https://www.editorandpublisher.com/stories/small-publishers-have-longer-runway-to-digital-but-they-still-need-to-take-off,201895.

123 Jacob, Mark, "Local News Outlets Boost Digital Subscriptions by About 50% in a Year," Local News Initiative, 16 Dec. 2020, https://localnewsinitiative.northwestern.edu/posts/2020/12/16/digital-subscriptions/index.html.

124 Alliance for Audited Media statement for six months ending 31 Mar. 2022, https://auditedmedia.com/.

125 Syre, David, "News Publication Comes to Bellingham," Bellingham PR & Comm,11 Aug. 2021, https://bellinghampr.com/new-daily-publication-in-bellingham/.

126 Metric Media, https://metricmedianews.com/.

127 Golino, Maria Alessandra, "Algorithms in Social Media Platforms," Institute for Internet & the Just Society, 24 Apr. 2021, https://www.internetjustsociety.org/algorithms-in-social-media-platforms.

128 Merrill , Jeremy B. and Will Oremus, "Five points for anger, one for a 'like': How Facebook's formula fostered rage and misinformation," The Washington Post, 26 Oct. 2021, https://www.washingtonpost.com/technology/2021/10/26/facebook-angry-emoji-algorithm/.

129 Zaitz, Les, et. al., "State legislator's private company poised to get another $180,000 from Malheur County," Malheur Enterprise, 21 May 2019, https://www.malheurenterprise.com/posts/5652/state-legislators-private-company-poised-to-get-another-180-000-from-malheur-county.

130 Zaitz, Les, et al., "Public Money, Private Empire: Greg Smith serves many public masters - for a price," Malheur Enterprise, 4 June 2019, https://www.malheurenterprise.com/posts/5697/public-money-private-empire-greg-smith-serves-many-public-masters-for-a-price.

131 Brown, Katrina, "Oregon Sheriff Declines to Investigate Local Paper for Basic Reporting," Courthouse News Service, 9 May 2022, https://www.courthousenews.com/oregon-sheriff-declines-to-investigate-local-paper-for-basic-reporting/.

132 "Investigation of Greg Smith wins top honors for the Enterprise," Malheur Enterprise, 19 May 2020, https://www.malheurenterprise.com/posts/7158/investigation-of-greg-smith-wins-top-honors-for-the-enterprise.

133 Davis, Rob, "Case Closed: In Oregon campaign investigations, 'I did not do it' is all it takes," 17 Sept. 2019, Malheur Enterprise, https://www.malheurenterprise.com/posts/6105/case-closed-in-oregon-campaign-investigations-i-did-not-do-it-is-all-it-takes.

134 Zaitz, Les, "Economic Development: Malheur County Officials struggle to tell what $900,000 bought," 2 Mar. 2022, Malheur Enterprise, https://www.malheurenterprise.com/posts/9454/economic-development-malheur-county-officials-struggle-to-tell-what-900-000-bought.

135 Chakradhar, Shraddha, "A local newspaper in Oregon punches above its weight. A politician it investigated wants to buy - and change - it," 31 Mar. 2022, Nieman Lab, https://www.niemanlab.org/2022/03/a-local-newspaper-in-oregon-punches-above-its-weight-a-politician-it-investigated-wants-to-buy-and-change-it/.

136 Report for America, https://www.reportforamerica.org/about-us/.

137 Staff reports, "The Spokesman-Review receives Report for America grant to add rural reporter," 13 Dec. 2021, The Spokesman-Review, https://www.spokesman.com/stories/2021/dec/12/spokesman-review-receives-report-for-america-grant/.

138 McClatchy Journalism Institute, https://www.guidestar.org/profile/84-2968843.

139 "The Daily Herald to Partner with Journalism Funding Partners," Journalism Funding Partners, 8 Sept. 2021, https://www.jfp-local.org/dailyheraldjoinsjfp.

140 "April 1, 2021 (Revised) Population of Cities, Towns and Counties, Used for Allocation of Selected State Revenues," State of Washington, https://www.ofm.wa.gov/sites/default/files/public/dataresearch/pop/april1/ofm_april1_population_final.pdf.

141 Edmonds, Rick, "Reeling in a federal boost for local journalism remains elusive," Poynter, 3 Apr. 2022, https://www.poynter.org/business-work/2022/local-journalism-sustainability-act-status-federal-funding-journalism/.

142 Dudley, Brier, "Attorney General Bob Ferguson on why local newspapers matter," Seattle Times, 22 Oct. 2021, https://www.seattletimes.com/opinion/attorney-general-bob-ferguson-on-why-local-newspapers-matter/.

143 Smith, Brad, "Technology and the Free Press: The Need for Healthy Journalism in a Healthy Democracy," Microsoft on the issues, 12 Mar. 2021, https://blogs.microsoft.com/on-the-issues/2021/03/12/technology-and-the-free-press-the-need-for-healthy-journalism-in-a-healthy-democracy/.

144 Benton, Joshua, "Australia's latest export is bad media policy, and it's spreading fast," Nieman Lab, 2 Feb. 2022, https://www.niemanlab.org/2022/02/australias-latest-export-is-bad-media-policy-and-its-spreading-fast/.

145 Karr, Timothy, "The Journalism Competition and Preservation Act Is Bad News for Local Journalism and Communities," Free Press, 2 Feb. 2022, https://www.freepress.net/news/press-releases/journalism-competition-and-preservation-act-bad-news-local-journalism-and.

146 "S. 1601: Future of Local News Act of 2021," Govtrack, 12 May 2021, https://www.govtrack.us/congress/bills/117/s1601/summary.

147 Hall, Dee J., "Advertising tax credit bill would help Wisconsin's local news outlets," Milwaukee Journal Sentinel, 3 Feb. 2022, https://www.jsonline.com/story/opinion/2022/02/03/advertising-tax-credit-bill-would-help-wisconsins-local-news-outlets/9305353002/.

148 Edmonds, Rick, "Reeling in a federal boost for local journalism remains elusive," Poynter, 29 Mar. 2022, https://www.poynter.org/business-work/2022/local-journalism-sustainability-act-status-federal-funding-journalism/.

149 Schmidt, Christine, "How Free Press convinced New Jersey to allocate $2 million for rehabilitating local news," Nieman Lab, 15 July 2019, https://www.niemanlab.org/2019/07/how-free-press-convinced-new-jersey-to-allocate-2-million-for-rehabilitating-local-news/.

150 Karr, Timothy, "New Jersey Funds the Civic Info Consortium, Recognizes the Vital Role Local News Plays During Crises," Free Press, 30 Sept. 2020, https://www.freepress.net/news/press-releases/new-jersey-funds-civic-info-consortium-recognizes-vital-role-local-news-plays.

151 Edmonds, Rick, "Reeling in a federal boost for local journalism remains elusive," Poynter, 29 Mar. 2022. https://www.poynter.org/business-work/2022/local-journalism-sustainability-act-status-federal-funding-journalism/.

152 Illinois Gov. J.B. Pritzker, "Gov. Pritzker Signs Legislation Creating the Local Journalism Task Force," 23 Aug. 2021 https://www.illinois.gov/news/press-release.23788.html.

153 Rieck, Kami, "State commission will explore ways to support local journalism," The Recorder, 28 Feb. 2021, https://www.recorder.com/State-commission-will-explore-ways-to-support-local-journalism-38831337.

154 Fisco, Alan, "Newspaper industry needs federal support to survive, grow again," The Yakima Herald-Republic, 7 Dec. 2021, https://www.yakimaherald.com/opinion/free_press/yfp/newspaper-industry-needs-federal-support-to-survive-and-grow-again/article_84574b21-0a38-5300-aa27-0a1379a36e20.html.

155 McChesney , Robert W., and John Nichols, "To Protect and Extend Democracy, Recreate Local News Media," 25 Jan. 2022, https://www.freepress.net/sites/default/files/2022-03/to_protect_democracy_recreate_local_news_media_final.pdf.

156 McChesney's books include "The Death and Life of American Journalism," "The Problem of the Media," "Corporate Media and the Threat to Democracy," "Rich Media, Poor Democracy," and "Telecommunications, Mass Media & Democracy."

Made in United States
Troutdale, OR
05/30/2024

20236395R00075